Now It's Personal:
The Truth About Health Care, Doctors, and Patients in 2009

Jeffrey B. English, MD
Director of Clinical Research
MS Center of Atlanta
Peachtree Neurological Clinic

Cover Illustrated by: Kaitlin E. English
Diane M. English

authorHOUSE®

AuthorHouse™
1663 Liberty Drive
Bloomington, IN 47403
www.authorhouse.com
Phone: 1-800-839-8640

First published by AuthorHouse 10/21/2009

ISBN: 978-1-4490-3257-9 (e)
ISBN: 978-1-4490-3256-2 (sc)

Printed in the United States of America
Bloomington, Indiana

This book is printed on acid-free paper.

Many thanks:

*To my wife who supported me through all those years of
training; who continues to support me every day.*

*To my children, who have missed seeing their
father at important events in life.*

*To my wife and children for allowing me the extra
time in a hectic schedule to write this book.*

*To William Waters, III for his review of the manuscript. Dr.
Waters could have saved health care years ago, but nobody asked.*

*Finally, thanks to the growers of fine coffee beans
and the entrepreneur's who have placed their product
on every street corner. You have all made the days
after being on-call much easier to handle.*

Contents

CHAPTER 1

Why It Became Personal

I started to write this book in early 2009. I planned on writing a book that would be published in 10 years looking back on the way we currently practice medicine in the United States of America, TODAY. I wanted to see how the care of patients changed over a 5-10 year period. The Senate and the House of Representatives had received marching orders to extend healthcare coverage to everyone in the United States. I knew that the Democrats had an overwhelming majority in both the House and Senate; I knew the President was a Democrat. I also knew that the President had stated many times before that he preferred socialized medicine as a model. However, I wanted this book to be completely devoid of politics and look just at patient care and see how it changed.

However, on Wednesday, July 22, 2009, the President MADE THIS PERSONAL! He held one of his many press conferences to push health care reform and wanted plans drafted by Congress by the end of July. He made completely uninformed statements about physicians and made allegations that were simply not true. Of course, up to that date, he was very vague about the actual plan. There were 5 different plans in progress, totaling over 1000 pages each. He did not shed any light that evening using any specifics. Despite every independent budget office analysis showing his reform would increase the deficit, statistics readily available all over the news and internet, he continued to tell the American people that this plan would be "revenue neutral." Although I found it offensive that he thought the American people were uneducated about the revenue statistics, I was willing to let that slide as that's "just politics."

He then proceeded to tell the American people that the cost of health care was going up because "physicians were ordering tests and doing procedures" specifically to make more money. He implied that our interests were in making money, not in providing excellent care to our patients. Well, this I could not stomach. I had never been as angry in my life as I was that night. His statement was incorrect and a direct assault on my fellow physicians. Physicians certainly weren't thinking of money when they were studying 18 hours a day in college and medical school, 6 - 7 days a week, while their friends were out having fun. There are many other easier ways to make money. Only an idiot would go to medical school, put themselves $200-350 thousand dollars in debt, just to make money as a physician. I have always had a HUGE problem with being accused of something I didn't do, even as a child. That's why I, like most physicians that night, was outraged by this accusation.

He, as usual, did not have any facts to back up his health care plan or his accusations. I don't expect the general US Citizen to understand the complexities of the health care industry. However, I do expect the President of the United States to have simple facts and examples to back up his overhaul plan of the health care industry. This is the industry, after all, that employs 1/6th of our workers and is the "life line" for all US citizens. He used pediatricians as an example of how physicians think of money when they make decisions for their patients. He stated that pediatricians decide to do tonsillectomies in order to make more money instead of treating patients with medications. Well, there are 2 problems with that statement. The obvious, most doctors would find it unethical to think of money instead of their patient's best interest first. The less obvious for those listening, pediatricians don't do tonsillectomies. They refer to surgeons who perform the procedure, so they themselves do not make more money. You would think that the President would at least come up with a remotely plausible example to drive home his point if it was true. I realized at that point that he was uninformed and that this was just a political issue for him. This is a personal issue for all the people (patients) in America.

I was also angry because his supposition that doctors were the primary drivers of the health care expense increase was incorrect. He rendered this lie to push through his plan, and left me up as a sacrificial lamb. Simply stated, in the 10 years prior to his statement, physician's reimbursement (or income) had not gone up. In fact, it had actually gone down. So, an informed individual would understand that if physicians were not making more money over 10 years, yet the cost of health care had been increasing, the money must have been going elsewhere. I only took 1 accounting class in college, but even I could figure that out.

The President is not uneducated, and I doubt he is truly uninformed. On the contrary, he is an extremely intelligent man. So, he decided to lie at the expense of physicians. I refuse to sit by and let that happen. Therefore, I changed the direction of this book and decided I really wanted to educate the public on how medicine really works in 2009. I wanted everyone to understand how and why doctors decide to order tests and how we really take care of patients. I will still be able to compare care in 10 years if I am still lucky enough to be taking care of patients who entrust their lives in my decisions and experience.

In reality, I should have expected the Healthcare Reformers to be uneducated about how health care is delivered in this Country. They have received briefings, but most of them have never run a physicians practice, a hospital, or an insurance company. Many are career politicians. I could not run IBM, but I know most of the regulations, laws and economic principles to run a medical practice. Some Senators have worked with health care lobbyists for years and have a tainted view on how the system works, seen through a lobbyist's eyes. Lobbyists have a specific agenda and are incapable of having an open mind. President Obama was a lawyer, a community organizer, and had a brief run in the Senate before becoming President. There is no way he could really understand how the system works. I don't fault him for that and I commend him on attempting to improve a system that needs adjustments. I do fault him for taking an incorrect crack at physicians who work most of their lives serving others often at the expense of their own personal lives. His statements are misleading and are misinformed, so I need to question whether improvement on the current system is in consideration at all.

I do not want to focus too much on the finances of the health care industry. That is 100% out of control of physicians; the Government has made sure of that. Although the destruction of healthcare since the advent of Medicare is a topic of which I am well versed, there are other authors who have written on this subject in much more depth. I do not want to make this an economic subject either, again a topic of which I am well versed. The best book on that subject (at least in 2009) is by the Harvard University Medical Economist, Regina Herzlinger, titled, "Who Killed Healthcare?" Yes, she is a nationally known health care economist, but no, her ideas are not being pushed by the Government. Why? Because she knows how the Government ruined health care already, how they are responsible for the escalating costs, and she certainly does not support more Government regulations as a way to "fix" the problem.

I had one political concept in the original idea for the book. The President had said he would build a "single payor system" if he were to draft the US healthcare system from scratch. He has stated that former Senator, Tom Daschle, had the best plan for fixing healthcare in the US. Summarizing Tom Daschle's book on healthcare reform, he recommended slowly passing bills, consecutively through Congress, incrementally moving medical care towards socialized medicine without people realizing what was going on. He too thought we were all just too dumb to understand their master plan. Why do so incrementally? Because, this would make it harder for people to revolt. They would revolt if they knew that the ultimate goal was to socialize medicine and ration care (largely based on age and one's ability to contribute to society). He felt the system needed to limit new developments in the future (as they tend to be more costly) even if these developments saved lives. While Tom Daschle did not make it as the Director of Health and Human Services and the new "Health Care Czar," the President still liked his plan. (If you have forgotten, Tom did not get to those positions because he had a little problem paying his taxes. He apparently thought he was able to draft a plan to control your health and life, 1/6th of the US economy, but could not figure out how to calculate his taxes. Maybe a well trained and educated accountant might have helped. If only someone would have shown him how to use the internet or the Yellow Pages to find one.) This is America. I am glad we all have the chance to voice our different opinions. I have no problem with Tom Daschle and President Obama wanting socialized medicine. I have no problem with those of you who agree with them. I have a huge problem with anyone being deceitful and slandering my profession as a means to an end.

So, I have every reason to believe that 5-10 years from now we (the patients) will miss "the way we used to practice medicine" and we will see a form of socialized medicine. If that happens, it will be a tragedy. However, I want everyone to understand that any mudslinging about physicians by the Government is misdirected. The problems in health care have almost nothing to do with "greedy doctors." Greedy doctors exist, just as greedy politicians exist. However, their limited existence doesn't even dent the problem the Government created years ago. The same Government is now asking the American People to trust them to fix the problems they created.

Chapter 2

Statistics

If any of the readers are politicians, you might want to skip this section. I know politicians don't want to let the truth or facts get in the way of their arguments.

The healthcare debate and comments became personal when the President essentially blamed physician greed, while on national T.V., as a major cause of healthcare costs rising. In the following chapters, we will examine why this is not the case and why it was just a political statement without much truth or basis. For his statement to be true, there has to first of all be one condition. In order for a physician to make a life altering decision on another human being, for the sole purpose of gaining more money, the physician has to directly gain financially from that decision. This is a simple truth and a fact that no one can debate. The physician also has to act unethically and against all he or she has been taught. The doctor has to act against their oath taken to protect all patients. Now, I don't think anyone in the United States actually believes that ALL physicians make ALL decisions based on how much revenue they themselves will receive, even if it's detrimental to the patient. So, we must be dealing with a subset of physicians to which the President was referring. The actual percent can be argued.

Let's take a look at the physician demographics in the United States. According the American Association of Medical Colleges (AAMC), in 2008 there were about 16,000 new medical students per year. There

7

are 4 years of medical school, so the total number is about 65-70,000 total medical students in the United States. They come from a very diverse background. About 45% of the students identify themselves as "White" while 55% identify themselves as "African American, Hispanic, or Other." 52.2% of the medical students identify themselves as "Male" while 47.8% identify themselves as "Female." According to the American Medical Association (AMA), in 2005 over 20% of the total physician population in the United States considered themselves of an "ethnic minority" and over 25% of the total physicians were women. These are just the facts. Unless all of the physicians of all genders and ethnic backgrounds came from the same neighborhood and went to the same schools, it stands to reason that they are a diverse group. Even if they all came from the same neighborhood, I think they would need the same parents in order to be non-diverse. It also stands to reason that they come from a diverse culture and upbringing with very diverse ethical and religious beliefs. Since neither medical school, nor residency, teach a standard of being unethical, it stands to reason that these people carry a variety of beliefs and ethical diversity into their professional lives.

Let us now analyze the belief that the current healthcare costs are so high because physicians try to "pad their pockets" and make money instead of doing right for the patient. I do not think this is simply the President's belief. I have heard many Congressmen and Congresswomen make the same argument.

In 2001, the AMA records indicated that 40% of all physicians were in salaried positions. Since that time, the number of physicians in salaried positions has steadily increased and is about 60% in 2009. We can throw out the 60% of physicians who are salaried because they get no more or less money based on the tests or treatment they order. Now we are down to 40% of the physicians that are causing healthcare costs to go up. Well, the 40% remaining do not all do procedures that bring in any revenue at all. 25% are primary care physicians. Some primary care physicians own an EKG machine. Rarely, they own a chest X-Ray machine. I think we can all agree the health care crisis is not believed to be caused by all those extra chest X-Rays and EKG's.

So, now we are down to about 30% of the physician pool that stands to gain whatsoever by ordering tests or by doing procedures. I think we can agree that as a general principle, physicians as a group are more ethical than some other professional groups like, for instance, politicians. They aren't all ethical, but most are driven to the field out of a desire to take care of their fellow man. As we examined above, physicians come from a variety of backgrounds, ethnic groups and have diversity in gender. So, unless the remaining 30% of physicians just happen to be from a uniformed ethnic group, cultural background, and gender, we need to throw out another 15-20% of these remaining 30% because they couldn't all just be greedy, unethical people.

So, now we are down to about 10-15% of physicians who hypothetically might be ordering tests for financial reasons. In order for that 10-15% to even make a dent in the healthcare cost increase, wouldn't they all need to be ordering the most expensive tests on a frequent basis? Wouldn't they need to be ordering these tests on a huge number of patient's? Is that possible? No! That test and group of doctors doesn't exist. If it did, the private insurance industry would have figured it out, exposed them, and shut them down years ago.

I do not believe for a second that the President's accusation about physicians is remotely true in the overwhelming majority of physicians. It just doesn't make sense and there are no facts to back up the thought that this is contributing to the health care crisis. I will readily admit that there is a small population of "bad physicians" that are bilking the system for money. I will readily admit that I am wrong if someone can prove to me that it is more than 1-2% of my colleagues. If I am wrong, I am not **so wrong** that this is responsible for the healthcare crisis in the United States. If the Healthcare Reformers set up a system by which all "bad doctors" are removed from the system, all financial incentives are removed from physicians in the system, the cost of healthcare won't go down one bit. They will then be faced with an increased deficit and they will only be able to control costs by limiting treatment and tests on everyone (a.k.a. rationing)!

CHAPTER 3

In Defense

In Defense of doctors, residents, medical students, and young students called to this profession.

Very few people go into medicine to "make money." There are a few, but there are many other ways to make a lot more money. During my first year in medical school, we had a lecture by an economist. He outlined the wealth of 2 people. One started working for minimum wage right out of high school. He got cost of living raises all throughout his career, saved 10% of his income for retirement, and retired at age 65. The other went on to college and medical school. Averages were used for the college and medical school debt. This person went on to 3 years of residency and became a primary care physician. When he started to make money at age 28, he also saved 10% of his income for retirement. Well, the primary care physician never caught up to the high school dropout and retired with less savings. I can assure you, medical school is not the road to financial security, job security maybe, but not wealth.

I went to Dartmouth Medical School. I was amazed at the types of people that filled up my 84 person class. We were from all kinds of backgrounds and were a variety of ages. There was a mix of race and about 50% of my class was female. Many came right out of college, but many had "real lives" before they returned to school. I believe the oldest member of our class was in his late 40's. Some were married; some had children. Most of us had to find a way to pay for medical school; very few had family money paying for medical school. Most of us took on debt with loans, but many took on debt with their lives, as they were on military scholarship.

Most of my classmates had stories similar to mine. My mother will tell you that at about age 4, after leaving Dr. Cannon's office in Spring Lake, New Jersey, I said to her, "I want to be a doctor." (Actually, it sounded more like "doctw" since I had a lisp.) This desire apparently stuck with me. I did very well in grammar school. By high school, I realized this was my definite path, so I worked harder than most students to get good grades.

Well, I finished in the top 10 of 150 students in high school and decided to go to Boston College. I studied long hours and did well in college. This did not come easy. Most of my friends were business majors. While my class load was large, my study hours were even larger and dwarfed the time my fellow business and pre-law majors were putting into studying. While they were out enjoying themselves, I was in Tip O'Neill's Library either studying or working to help pay for BC. This is a common theme, you see. Your friends are out having fun, while the premedical student, medical student, or resident is studying or on-call. (Actually, this is a theme that has not ended now 10 years into practice compared to my friends.)

The studying and extra work at BC paid off. While many of my classmates had to drop pre-med due to the workload, I succeeded. I was accepted to several medical schools, both in California (my home state) and private schools. Despite being accepted to UCLA, which I still consider one of the greatest medical institutions in the country, I fell in love with Dartmouth Medical School in New Hampshire. Dartmouth is private and I took on an additional $95 thousand principal loan debt to add to my $15 thousand from BC. I could have come out of the University of California with a debt of about $30,000 for both college and medical school. I instead took on a larger debt to follow my dreams at the schools I felt would better prepare me for the life I chose.

Like many of my fellow medical school classmates, I came from a humble background and had no financial backing. My parents did not pay a nickel for college or medical school. My father left law school to become an actor, first in New York, and then in Los Angeles. Were it not for his parents help, we often would not have had food on the table. This is a very common story of medical students as we are not all from privileged backgrounds. I had medical school friends that were Latino from California who took on debt with a goal of returning home to take care of migrant farm workers. I can tell numerous stories about medical students, like my friend from California, who went to medical school for noble reasons. It was "a calling," not a job. The people who returned to medical school from other professions, with established careers, were certainly not thinking of it as a way to become rich. Statistically, these people lost money.

You graduate from medical school around age 25, if you go there right out of college. You finally get a job between ages 28-34 and you get to finally pay back your debt, little by little. By this time, your friends from college have been working for 10-15 years. Most have never been "on call", and are having fun while you spend countless hours in libraries or hospitals. Many of your friends have saved as much money as you accumulated in debt. Most physicians don't complain about this. We understand that it was a chosen path, but it's not a path chosen to make more money than others.

My Further Personal Background

During my 9 years of private practice in Atlanta, I have been intimately involved with many aspects of the health care industry. This includes hospitals and their associations, the insurance industry, and the pharmaceutical industry. I have spoken with leaders in those industries. I have worked in a private practice group as well as an employed physician at a non-profit organization that takes care of patients with multiple sclerosis.

So, you can see, I not only know the enemies (I mean players) in the system, I also know what makes them tick and how they control the laws and the flow of money in the system. Because I know them, I have less than optimistic outlook on what they will do in the near future, especially the government.

I do not recommend my lifestyle to anyone! I say this all the time. I greatly enjoy doing what I do. For me, like most physicians, it was a "calling." However, it is not for most people and my hours and lifestyle are not compatible with what most people view as a "good way of life." I am driven by 3 things daily. One, I expect myself to provide the best care possible, no matter what sacrifice that entails. Two, I do my best not to get sued inappropriately. This is on my mind all the time. It does force me to do things that I would otherwise not do (like order tests and admit unnecessarily to the hospital, for example.) It forces me to spend ungodly hours documenting my thought process and why I have recommended certain courses of action. We have computerized medical records and can link directly into facilities where most of the tests we order are done. In the "olden days" it could take up to a week to get test reports (like an MRI report). Well, I can get most of them right away. I just need to know when the test is done and I can log onto the computer system and see the results, often before the interpreting doctor has even seen the test. This requires my staff to work harder, as we need to track many tests. Three, and most importantly for my sanity, I try to get home enjoy my family when I am not on call.

I wake up at about 5 a.m. daily. I get to the office at about 630 a.m. For an hour, I track down tests, review test results, and make patient decisions based on those tests. I fill out patient forms for insurance companies, work and disability. I do the same thing from about 4 p.m. to 530 p.m. I schedule patients from 730 a.m. to 330 p.m. and I finish, on a good day, by 4 p.m. to do my paperwork. I have no free time in between. At 12 p.m. to 1 p.m., I usually do not schedule patients. I use this time to see an urgent patient if need be, or get caught up on my paperwork. I also run the Research Department at our MS Center, so I often have research requirements during that time. (Mr. President, I generate no money for this work. I do not ask for sympathy, just an admission that there is no financial payment for this extra work. It is done for the patient's benefit.)

I am on call every Tuesday night. If a patient needs to be seen right away, like if a new stoke occurs, I go to the hospital. If it is not emergent, the hospital physician and I discuss the course of treatment and the patient is seen the next day. I answer phone calls from patients from our general neurology practice (8 doctors worth) and the patients from the MS Center (about 4,000 patients). I get up the next day, no matter how much sleep I get, and work a full day.

I do not do this for money. I do not recommend anyone, DO THIS FOR MONEY. I also caution everyone who is a proponent of socialized medicine to accept the fact that doctors will not work like this under socialized medicine. Academic physicians don't work like this. Government doctors do not work like this. I remember as a medical student rounding at 430 p.m. in the intensive care unit at one of the VA hospitals. The Government employed physician each day would look down at his watch. In the middle of rounds, before we had seen all the patients, he would say, "Government employee, it's time to go home." He would then turn around and go home, leaving the rest of the rounds up to the medical students and residents to finish alone. I kid you not.

CHAPTER 4

Socialized Medicine

Socialized Medicine- The Case for or Against

Isn't America Great! We are all free to have our own opinions and are free to express them. I am more than happy to discuss the merits of our system versus socialized medicine with anyone. I have no ill will for those who understand socialized medicine and feel this is the way to go. What I have a problem with is anyone who has an uninformed opinion on socialized medicine, or our current private system for that matter. The purpose of this chapter is not to sway your opinion, it's to inform.

I want to reiterate why I think that the current health care debate is not truly a "debate," but the start of socialized medicine. The President has clearly stated the following. He has stated that he feels socialized medicine is the best model for health care. He has stated that the Great Britain and Canadian models are ones that we should strive to duplicate. He has stated that he believes we can get to socialized medicine incrementally. He has stated that Tom Daschle had the best health care reform model. Tom Daschle's book on reform shows how to incrementally get socialized medicine. So, if you follow the paths of the President's own words, one has to logically conclude that he is laying the foundation for socialize medicine incrementally, no? These are his words, not mine. I can be wrong, but it seems like the logical conclusion.

In many of my suppositions and examples, I refer to the future as socialized medicine. We may not end up exactly where Canada is, but we may get close. (Of course, where Canada "is" is not where it "will be" when WE are where Canada currently "is." Since they can't afford their system, the one many want to emulate, the Canadians are changing the system all the time. They decrease the resources available to patients frequently. Canada has about 35 million people and Great Britain has about 75 million. The United States has over 300 million. Our task to do what they have failed to do, will be much harder.)

Unfortunately, medical care is a limited resource. No one can argue otherwise. No society can afford to provide ALL CARE TO EVERYONE. No one in Great Britain or Canada will argue against this point. In socialized medicine, basic healthcare is guaranteed to everyone. There is no promise when or where you will get that care. The government decides what "basic health care" means and provides it accordingly. When they have less money, they provide less care. They start by limiting the resource, or the care they provide, in an obvious fashion. The 20 year old gets his blood pressure medication, while the 77 year old is denied surgery, for example, that will extend her life or prevent disability for 10 more years. The cancer patients get "treated" but there is delay in diagnosis. The delay provides less tests and treatments which saves the system money. Many young and old people die who would otherwise have survived had they been diagnosed and treated earlier. Tom Daschle does not deny this in his book. That is just collateral damage in the system to provide "basic care to everyone."

In the current US system, people are treated as individuals. We look at one person and decide what is best for them. We use statistics on appropriate care and how others have responded to our treatments, but we are free to deviate. Our system is fast and we diagnose disease much quicker than our socialized counterparts. The collateral damage is that some people can't afford this care. Doctors often see people for free, but they have to jump through hoops to do so and cannot openly agree to see them for free or it's a Medicare violation. (More discussion on that later.) Hospitals get tax breaks to care for the uninsured. Drug companies often give free medications. Private insurance companies increase their prices to cover costs provided to people for free. Despite the free care from the industry, some people go without care.

If you are a proponent of socialized medicine, keep this in mind; people will still die and won't get covered. Even preventative medicine does not save much money. 80% of all health care dollars are spent in the last year of life. Preventative care delays heart attacks and death, for instance, but it does not cost us less. The heart attack will still happen since we haven't cured death yet. We could "fix" our health care system by adjusting in how it is delivered.

President Obama asked for initial plans in healthcare reform by the end of July, 2009. He wants to pass a Bill to cover healthcare for everyone to be signed into law by the end of 2009. The Democratic leaders in Congress have promised such a plan. The US health care industry is 1/6th of the entire economy. I don't think my brain can handle the actual number of people that work in the industry as a whole. Insurance companies, hospitals, health care professionals, pharmaceutical companies, litigation/contract attorneys and companies that deliver products to the system all have employees. That is a staggering number of people whose jobs are about to be greatly affected, with some grave sacrifices. The system is very complex and enormous and employs a large segment of our population. So, I think my concerns for eventual socialized medicine are real when they want to change this over a 6-8 month time period.

There's another interesting tidbit of information. I recently heard a member of the British Parliament speak. He said that Great Britain has about 1.5 million employees in their National Health Service. That makes them the 3rd largest employer in the world, just behind the Chinese Red Army. More than half of the employees are administrators. That means that less than half of the employees are doctors or nurses that provide direct care. We all understand that once you create a government position, it is hard to get rid of it, if not impossible. Great Britain has a population of 75 million; the US population is over 300 million. That means that if we duplicate their system, we will have over 6 million healthcare employees in the US and less than half of them will be doctors or nurses. I refuse to believe that this will decrease costs.

The facts are really to the contrary and people will pay more for their healthcare in the form of taxes and receive less care for their dollars.

Our Medicaid Experience in Georgia as a Window into Government Involvement

My general neurology practice no longer has a contract with Medicaid in the State of Georgia. Before you start thinking that we are "money hungry, fee schedule reviewing, and evil," I want you to know that we still see these patients for reduced cost in the hospital and still see them for free in the office. When we take care of a Medicaid patient in the hospital, they reimburse us 75% of the regular fees paid to their contracted physicians. (Medicaid obviously does not restrict who sees the patient in the hospital. If we are the only doctors available, they want their patients taken care of, so they just reduce the payments.) When we follow-up with them in the office, it ends up being for free. This is not a violation of our Medicare contract since we bill them but end up not collecting any fees. We promise to take care of them until they find an outpatient physician who is contracted with Medicaid.

Why did we decide to see Medicaid patients for free or for a reduced reimbursement? Well, there were 2 reasons.

Number one, it cost us more in manpower and time to collect money from Medicaid than we were being paid. The cost was higher than the reimbursement. This is the same reason many physicians do not take Medicare in the U.S. When we were paid, it was more often than not extremely delayed.

Number two, more importantly, we felt it unsafe to practice under their model. Very often, a procedure that we felt was urgent would take 3-4 weeks to obtain. This was often far outside the appropriate window. Emergencies seen in the office were no problem, as we just admitted them directly to the hospital. The urgencies were the problem. We were liable if they died or became disabled while waiting for the test. There was no easy method for getting tests done expediently.

I will give you two examples and "final straws" in my case. I saw a 25 year old female in the office with a new onset headache of 1-2 weeks duration. She was having right arm numbness and weakness. She needed a brain MRI. Since the disease duration was over a week, I did not feel it emergent to admit her directly to the hospital. The MRI could be done in 2-5 days. Well, after a week of waiting for approval, after several phone calls to Medicaid administrators, they told me the MRI request was going to committee review and the review could take up to a month. That was very unsafe for the patient. She may have been having strokes, could have a brain tumor, or could have a life threatening vascular malformation. I called her and met her at the hospital. Medicaid turned a $600 outpatient MRI into a $10,000 hospital bill. I had to do it for the patient and for medico-legal reasons. I was not willing to subject my patients to similar risks and was not willing to subject myself to further malpractice risks. You can't sue Medicaid for delaying a test. You can sue a doctor for delay of a test even if he or she ordered it on time.

I had another Medicaid patient that required a medical treatment every 3 months. This treatment enabled him to eat and swallow better and greatly reduced his daily pain. The medication and procedure were "approved" under Medicaid guidelines. The medication cost my office $1,200 to purchase every 3 months. For that $1,200 office expense, Medicaid agreed to pay approximately $1,100. For my technical services, we were to be paid $250. So, every 3 months, although we knew ahead of time that we would lose $100 for the medication purchase, we would net about $150. Since the procedure and medication were so helpful, we provided the treatments.

Well, we were not paid for the first treatment by the time the second treatment was due. We proceeded with the second treatment as we expected to eventually be paid for an approved therapy. The same thing happened, however, when the 3rd treatment was given. At that point, we were out $3,600 for the medicine and $750 for the procedure. We had to stop the treatments. The Medicaid offices could not tell us if or when we would be paid. Eventually, after a year, we were paid for the first treatment. We had to write off the rest of the bill. Unfortunately, the patient suffered the most, since he was unable to continue with a life altering therapy. If it was legal, I would have been happy for him to bring in the medication and I would have injected it for free. However, Medicaid did not allow for him to pick up the medication elsewhere and it would be illegal for me to inject the medication for free.

For physicians to survive in a private practice model, delay in reimbursement has huge implications. 50-75% of the revenue that goes into a private practice office goes to overhead. Overhead is rent, employee's salaries, and the benefits employees receive, including their health care coverage. These offices are not huge corporations with cash reserve. Their bank accounts are very small and they cannot sustain much of a delay in payments. I am concerned that the "public option plan" in discussion will look a lot like Medicaid in Georgia. If payments are delayed to private practice offices, they will not be able to keep their doors open. Employees will have delayed pay checks, then they will be let go, then the offices doors will close.

My biggest fear for the future is that medicine in the United States will be practiced in this fashion. We will be forced to wait too long for procedures and tests which will lead to increased death and disability, all preventable in our current system. The details of the particular patient become irrelevant with Government control, as guidelines are set up for a population not an individual. Since they are not mentioning malpractice reform at all, doctors will still be liable for patient outcomes even though they follow a protocol set up by the Government. We all will agree that getting through to someone in any Government run industry is nearly impossible. I do not believe the Government system will be able to handle phone calls efficiently, while we now can explain the need for procedures and tests to the insurance industry in minutes. There is not a single person reading this book that would disagree. I fear walls and road blocks set up by a bureaucracy, phone trees that are endless, and websites that are impossible to navigate. My office will not be able to employ enough people to get emergencies or urgencies handled through the Government run system. We will, therefore, not even be able to try and the patient will suffer. We know this will happen because we have models showing us the failure. We only have to look to Medicaid, Medicare and the VA System in the United States, and to the systems in Canada and Great Britain for proven failed examples.

The same proportion of people will get neglected, the system will be very inefficient, and this will affect you every time you seek medical care. People will still die and become disabled. Those are facts. Again, look to the stated examples that have proven this over and over. Under the systems proposed in Congress thus far, care will still be restricted.

CHAPTER 5

The Government- Truths and Misperceptions

The Government Regulations Make It Illegal for Physicians to Provide Free or Reduced Fees for Care

It is hard to believe, but true. The exact body that is going to fix the medical problem has made it criminal for physicians to reduce fees or give free care to those unable to pay regular fees. In the past, before these regulations, it was not uncommon for physicians to accept pay based on a patient's ability to cover a bill. It was not uncommon at all for physicians to accept non-monetary items instead of money for their services (like a chicken or home grown vegetables). Yes, it was also not uncommon for a physician to care of patients for free.

Now, once a physician agrees to take Medicare, or signs a Medicare contract, all of that is illegal. The way the government looks at it is, "If you can accept $20 for a visit from someone, it is actually stealing if you take the $60 agreed upon in your Medicare contract." Remember, Medicare equals the Government. So, in the case above, they look at the doctor as a criminal because he "stole" an extra $40 from the Government.

Once Medicare set these rules, what do you think private insurers decided to do? Well, my Blue Cross and Aetna contracts, for example, have similar clauses. They do not want me to provide a service for free or at half priced to one person while charging them double. This is another example where an industry lobby worked in cahoots with Uncle Sam to benefit themselves. In essence, they made it illegal for physicians to alter pay scales or provide free care. There are penalties for doing this. If a doctor ignores those contracts in order to help a patient who is poor or has fallen on hard times, there are hefty fines. Legal action for such "criminal behavior" is also possible.

We are allowed to give a small discount. We can justify a small discount, usually 10%. Patients who pay cash do not require billing, so the cost of the service is less. We can also write off a bill if the patient does not pay. There is no law that requires us to send a patient's bill to a collection agency. We just have to show an effort to collect the money.

I will give an example of a real life situation. Some states and insurance companies have approved Botox for intractable, frequent migraine headaches in patients who have failed all routine medications. Some insurance companies and States have not. A physician may want to provide the treatment, let's say for $300 cash, if a patient's insurance company won't approve the treatment. If the usual cost to the insurance company is $750, then the reduced payment in cash is a violation of the doctor's insurance contracts. If the other 10 Insurance companies find out, they can legally ask the physician to reimburse them for the difference between the $300 and $750 on ALL PATIENTS RETROACTIVELY THAT RECEIVED THE TREATMENT! This example has actually happened. So, the patient just suffers even though numerous medical studies indicate that, in the correct patient, this treatment reduces the frequency and severity of headaches by 50%. It is also cost effective. These patients tend to use emergency rooms 5-10 times a year, at the cost of $1000-3000 per visit. The Botox treatments are given 4 times a year for about $750 per treatment (about $600 of which covers the cost of the Botox). The monetary difference is $3000 per year for Botox treatments and $5000-30,000 per year for ER visits.

Thanks Uncle Sam!

Medicare Fraud and Abuse

"Fraud" and "abuse" are other terms the US Government likes to throw around. The Reformers use these terms to justify a takeover of the system. They use these terms to make you believe that the health care costs are skyrocketing because doctors and hospitals are running around charging false claims and performing unnecessary procedures. They are correct, partly. As I admitted, there are bad people in every business. We just learned that the SEC (Securities and Exchange Commission) allowed Mr. Madoff to run the largest Ponzi Scheme in US history. Despite repetitive warnings for over 10 years, Mr. Madoff continued to swindle $ millions from unsuspecting people. This too happens in medicine. There are some physicians who do up-charge or create patients that don't exist for money. There are business schemes set up to do the same, some run by physicians and some with physicians as partners with business criminals. These are rare occurrences, but you have all seen these schemes revealed before on TV shoes like 20/20.

However, the "fraud and abuse" numbers they give you involve fraud in only a percentage of cases. This is another great example of how the Government "criminalizes innocent Americans" as the numbers they give you are misleading.

Let me explain some of this fraud. In order to understand, you must first understand how doctors and hospitals bill for their services. I give a talk that discusses medical economics. I have given this talk many times in front of business people. I am always amused as I look at their faces as they seem shocked. Their faces say, "Come on, this can't be true. Business doesn't run like that; if it did, we'd go bankrupt or never get anything done."

A physician essentially bills based on a series of codes, called E & M codes. Seems very simple at the outset, but like everything created by bureaucrats, it is very complex. When you look at your medical charge sheet at the doctor's office, you will see codes for a new patient visit that end in the numbers 1-5. A follow-up visit code ends in the numbers 1-3. Well, the lower the code, the easier and, therefore, cheaper the service.

Coding seems simple, right? A doctor takes care of a complex medical problem, there is a higher payment. Well, it's not that simple. As a matter of fact, there are numerous courses teaching physicians the rules that constitute each code number. When I was a resident, I took these courses in each of my 5 years as an intern, resident, and fellow. I still get confused. Every computer based medical record tries to help the doctor code correctly. There are thousands of programs on PDA's that help with coding. I am in charge at my office making sure the other physicians and nurse practitioners understand the coding rules. We have a separate partner that reviews charts randomly for each physician to make sure they are doing things correctly. He is our Compliance Officer. Each of my associates has also taken one of these courses many times. We still have difficulty figuring out how to comply with the rules of coding.

The level of coding should be easy. A very difficult patient, one with a life threatening emergency, or one with multiple problems, should get a higher code and payment. That seems simple. But there are rules about what is considered an emergency, an urgency, and how many problems constitute "many problems."

Where they get you (where it gets tough) is in the documentation. When you first lay eyes on the patient, you have no idea how complex the situation might be. When you take a history and do a physical exam, you are acquiring data. At the very end, after you have finished the exam and finished gathering information, you are ready to figure out the correct code. After you figure out at the very end how severe the problem is and how many problems you will be handling, you then need to go back through your whole documentation that led up to your conclusion and make sure you have documented everything correctly. You could have just saved someone's life in the emergency room, taken them for a cardiac catheterization for a life threatening coronary artery narrowing, but if you didn't document correctly, you have committed "fraud" when you bill for the highest level.

To understand how complicated this is, one needs to know how our thought process flows. Our notes and thought process go in a sequential order and contain the following sections:

Chief Complaint
Past Medical History
Family History
Social History
Medications

Allergies
Review of Systems
Physical Exam
Labs
Assessment and Plan

We go through this sequence on every patient. The Chief Complaint through the Labs sections takes the majority of our time. However, the Assessment and Plan determine the eventual code level. If the code is a high level based on the Assessment and Plan, then the documentation for the other sections must comply with a high code even though the physician has already completed those sections. You see, coding is actually backwards compared with how we work and this leaves room for error.

All along the way, there is information (or bullets) that must be documented in order to achieve certain codes. My favorite is the Review of Systems section. All physicians agree that this is the least important part of the patient encounter, but it causes improper coding the most. There are 14 systems in the body to review, from cardiovascular to psychiatric. For a complete, high level visit, you need to document information from 12 systems. Now remember, it's not enough that you obtain the information, if it's not documented, the Government assumes you didn't do it. The more complex a patient presentation, the more questions we ask anyway. Now, remembering how many systems you must write in your note in order to get a certain billing level is more difficult. It is difficult, especially when you are in a hurry to save someone's life in the hospital, to remember the correct documentation. In a true emergency, you must do the note later, after the fact, and it's even harder to remember what you did or said when you were in a hurry.

So, how does "fraud" occur? The "bullets" and documentation actually determine the code. When your chart is reviewed by Medicare, they look at the billing code and documentation. Even if the physical service you provided meets a level 5, e.g. you saved a patient from an emergent heart attack, you actually committed fraud in their eyes if you missed just one necessary "bullet." You saved their life, but your note may have missed one Review of System bullet. You forgot to mention anything about the patient's memory or sleep pattern, so you committed "fraud." The level 5 becomes a level 4 because you only documented 11 out of 14 Systems.

What happens in true practice is that most physicians "down code." They are afraid of being audited, most really can't remember the 100 rules of coding each time they see someone, so they just down code. This brings up 2 interesting facts. It is still Medicare Fraud to "down code." Even though you saved Medicare money by charging less, you can still be fined for "Medicare Fraud." Physicians know this is fraud, but feel it is safer. That's right, the rules are so complex, that we err on receiving less money for our services hoping that "down coding fraud" will look better than "up-coding fraud." After thousands of hours studying to get into a good college, studying to get into medical school, and working un-Godly hours in post medical school training, we can't understand how to code correctly. We charge less for our service than we deserve out of fear of the Government.

When a physician's office is audited by Medicare, they will review a finite number of charts. If they find up-coding in a certain percentage of charts, they will extrapolate that it occurred in the same percentage of all Medicare patients, and levy a fine based on that extrapolated number. They say that you owe them money. Well, as I said, most physicians down code. So, what does Medicare do with the money they owe you? If the system was fair, they would owe you some money for the charts you down coded and you would owe them money for the charts you up coded. Obviously, that doesn't happen. They just look at what you owe them, call it "fraud," and take money back. The fact may be that your errors in billing may have saved them a ton of money, but they still call it fraud and take money back.

Hospitals face a similar problem. They are paid by Medicare based on codes as well. These codes are based on a diagnosis. Makes sense, right? Medicare should pay more for an acute heart attack that requires bypass surgery than a urinary tract infection that requires only a day in the hospital with IV antibiotics. It is more complex, however. Some visits are actually billed like an extended outpatient visit if, for example, the patient is in the hospital less than 24 hours. Some diagnosis codes are allowed in the hospital and some are not. Some diagnosis are allowed as inpatient visits, some fall under the short stay visits, while others are only allowed as outpatient visits.

The physician seems to be required when they admit a patient to the hospital to be able to see into the future. The physician must know how long the patient will be in the hospital, even though they are not sure of the final diagnosis or treatment. A patient may be admitted with a simple urinary tract infection and go home the next day, or they may have a subsequent infection that spreads into the blood requiring weeks of antibiotics. If the admission code used for the latter patient is the same as the former patient, the billing for the hospital stay is still considered "fraud." Both of these patients can look exactly the same in the ER. Remember, they use the term "fraud" based on codes and documentation, not on what truly happens. The Medicare auditors do not care what happened, whether or not complications occurred, they only care about the codes and how much money they can ask the hospital to return.

In the hospital, very often patients are seen by many physicians. If, for example, 5 physicians see a patient and one uses the wrong diagnosis code, the whole stay is considered "fraudulent." If that hospital stay costs $20,000 and the correct bill should have been for $18,000 based on the one physician's documentation error, Medicare will consider the fraud to be $20,000, not $2,000 (the difference between $20,000 and $18,000). That's why you hear hospitals owing Medicare $50 million after an audit. This is essentially extortion by the Federal Government because they are "judge and jury" and the hospital will get no benefit from the money Medicare may owe the hospital in other cases.

So, don't believe all the numbers when they tell you about "Medicare Fraud."

Preventable Medical Complications

I would like to discuss the misnomer they call "preventable medical complications." Medicare wants to now refuse to pay for any medical illnesses that they consider preventable in hospitalized patients. This is the latest attempt at extortion from the hospitals by the Government. I don't care how educated the reader, we all completely understand that there are potential complications in EVERY medical procedure or illness, and a certain percentage of patients will have these complications no matter what the physician or hospital does for prevention. For instance, if you have a total knee or hip replacement, despite precautions, a certain percentage of patients will develop blood clots in their legs. Surprise, surprise; if one keeps a leg from moving normally for 3-7 days, blood flow slows down and a clot can develop. I have had patients develop these same clots driving on a long trip to Disneyworld. (Watch out Mickey Mouse, Uncle Sam and Medicare are coming to get you for all the medical complications you cause!) If we put these patients on blood thinners and move them around with artificial machines, the rates of clots go down, but are not zero. The blood thinners, by the way, can cause other complications, such as bleeding, that can be life threatening. No matter what, complications are going to happen. Medicare has decided that these clots should be prevented, with the maneuvers and medications mentioned. Medicare is now working on a plan to deny payment for the entire procedure and hospitalization if one of these clots develop, regardless of whether or not the medications were used for prevention. They do not just want to get repaid if the medications aren't used, but in everyone. Sound familiar.

Let's give one last ridiculous example, although the examples are endless. Medicare believes that they should not have to pay for any hospitalization where a patient wears a catheter and develops a urinary tract infection. These are preventable, right? If there is no catheter, there is no chance for a catheter induced infection. Never mind the fact that many patients need these catheters, are bed bound, and urinating all over themselves. Never mind that skin breakdown, infection, sepsis and death are more likely in a patient lying in urine. Let's say a patient has a stroke, cannot get out of bed, and can't even tell you they need to urinate. They need a catheter to prevent skin breakdown and infection from urinating all over themselves. Let's say their stroke stay in the hospital would have been 7 days. They get a urinary tract infection on day 7 and they are treated and released to a rehabilitation facility on day 9 in order to get the infection under control before transfer. Well, this is not a preventable error, it's a well known complication. The infection caused the patient to stay 2 more days. Medicare feels the hospital should not be paid for any of the 9 days, not just the 2 extra days.

Readmission Rates

If you are surprised by the whole idea of denying Medicare payments for those normal complications, let's look at the most recent lie. Medicare has recently gone on the attack wanting to deny payments for anyone re-admitted to a hospital within 30 days of discharge. For example, if a patient is discharged after a 10 day stay for congestive heart failure and they return within 30 days for the same reason, Medicare does not want to pay for the second admission. They argue that if the hospital, nurses and physicians had done their jobs, the patient would have been cured the first time. They feel proper care the first time and proper follow-up as an outpatient would have prevented the need for the second admission. This would be a great money saver for Medicare. Instead of having to pay for 2 hospitalizations, they would only pay for one.

Well, I got news for you Uncle Sam, SICK PEOPLE ARE SICK! HOSPITALS TAKE CARE OF THE SICKEST OF THE SICK PEOPLE! The sicker someone is, the harder it is to cure them. I spoke to one of the Kaiser administrators in Georgia, whose data shows that Medicare is just flat out wrong. Kaiser is a self contained system and they do better than anyone at making sure, to the best of their ability, that people stay healthy and transition to and from the outpatient and hospital arenas efficiently. They make sure that patients have appropriate follow-up when they leave the hospital. They set up a program for the sickest 20% of their hospital patients. These patients not only leave the hospital with detailed follow-up, they have phone interactions several times before their 2 week follow-up. They have direct phone numbers to a health care provider. Despite this extra care, their re-admission rate for the sickest patients is near 100%. Kaiser does a great job setting follow-up care for all of their hospital patients. For the other 80% of the patients, their readmission rate is about 12-15%. Are the sickest patients readmitted because the Kaiser doctors did not set up discharge or follow-up correctly? No, they are readmitted because SICK PEOPLE ARE SICK AND SICKNESS IS MOST OFTEN NOT CURABLE!

Here's a concern for the future: If we accept the fact that most of our health care dollars are spent on a small percentage of really sick people and the hospitals are further financially dis-incentivized to take care of sick people, who will take care of them? You can easily see how a hospital would benefit greatly if they just took care of easy patients. Instead of a system by which you attract the best physicians and the best facilities to take care of the more complicated patients, we may set up a system that does the opposite. It's not a greed thing. If the hospital can't afford a staff, can't afford good doctors, it shuts down. That's plain and simple!

CHAPTER 6

Those Evil and Expensive Tests- that save our lives

If you watch TV now, you will hear the people in Washington, DC demonizing medical tests. They infer that tests cost too much money. Because of tests, the health care costs are skyrocketing. Those demons we call physicians are ordering these tests and they are NOT NECESSARY!

Well, how would you feel if the PGA all of a sudden told Tiger Woods that he could not use a Driver, a 7 iron, or a putter? He could use all the other clubs in his bag, but not those clubs. Well, Tiger might just do alright with less tools for his trade, so let's make it more difficult. Let's take away all the modern Nike clubs and give him a set of blades from 1930. Do you really think even Tiger could play at the same level? Do you think it would be as much fun watching the Masters on TV? (Well, I suspect it would be fun to watch for comical reasons.)

Medical technology is amazing. I marvel every day at the inventions and tools at my finger tips that make it easier to diagnose and save lives. Let's be honest, how can tests or procedures be bad in and of themselves if they save lives and help us get a quicker return to our families and everyday lives? The politicians not only want you to believe that these tests are evil and unnecessary; they want you to believe that the only way to cure our health care problems is to limit the tests. Let's say it in a different way. They want you to believe that we will all get better health care globally if we just limit the use of tests, drugs and procedures designed to save our lives. Does that make sense?

Here's an idea. Instead of getting rid of the tests, let's make them more affordable. We have $400 laptops, why can't we have $200 MRI's? Well, we can. If they fixed the economics of healthcare, not revolutionize healthcare itself, we could bring the costs WAAAAAY down! An MRI at my hospital costs $2500. The same MRI at my office costs $500. If you allowed a free market in healthcare, all the MRI's would go down in price. This is simple supply and demand economics. A certain number of people need a test or procedure (that is the demand). The Government can't change the true demand, or the number of people who really need a medical test. They do, however, already control the supply. They limit the places where tests can be done; they limit the numbers of tests by regulations. If there was an MRI on every street corner, for example, the cost of the machine would go way down and you could pay about $100-200 for the MRI you need for your health. Instead, a small number of MRI's are allowed in the country, so the machine costs $1-2 million dollars and the test costs $2500.

I wish I could impress upon the reader how truly amazing medical technology has become. The things we can do now, the speed and accuracy with which we can do it, and the benefit patients receive in life extension and quality of life is leaps and bounds above what we could do compared to 40 years ago when I was born. Every 5-10 years, we improve upon the past for the benefit of human life. We don't move as fast as the computer industry. The joke always goes, "as soon as you walk out of the store with your new computer, it's outdated." But, we advance at a pretty amazing speed and the technology and developments are largely invented in the United States.

Those "evil tests" are a major part of medical advancement. We now do things faster, more accurate and more precise. By the way, most importantly, these tests have made the diagnosis and treatment of patients FAR SAFER. They have decreased complications greatly. They have reduced the costs of providing care in many areas. The bottom line, which NO POLITICIAN CAN REFUTE, is that the quicker we diagnose a medical problem, the better the patient outcome. They also can't refute the fact that the safer we are able to diagnose and treat a problem, the less we run the risk of hurting the patient while trying to save them. This saves lives, and money!

Let's use MRI's for example. Some genius (actually a whole group of them) figured out that if you put a human body in a magnetic field, connect it to a computer program (developed by another set of geniuses), you could get spectacular pictures of the inside of the body. The technology is so developed that the computer can decide how to look at specific parts of the body while ignoring others, for instance it can look at blood vessels only. We can make a diagnosis of complex problems in 30 minutes. In the past, some of these diagnosis were made only by cutting people open, sometimes when they were alive and at other times after they had died.

When a person presents to my hospital with a relatively sudden onset of difficulty speaking, statistically they are likely to have a stroke. If you were in Vegas, this would be a good bet, not a sure bet, but a good one statistically. However, there are other diseases that can present in the same fashion that require immediate treatment to prevent death and disability. Patients can have infections that require immediate antibiotics. Herpes encephalitis is an example (from the cold sore version we all have in our body). A stroke patient and a patient with herpes encephalitis can look exactly the same in the emergency room. They both can have difficulty speaking, may or may not have a fever, and their CT scans of the brain can look the same (or be completely normal). Herpes encephalitis is over 80% fatal if not treated with an antiviral medication. It is almost 100% curable if treated promptly. The earlier we treat it, the far better the preservation of the patient's brain (mostly memory and personality). An MRI is accurate in diagnosing stroke in over 98% of patients within a few hours of symptom onset. It also can almost always help us tell the difference between the 2 diagnosis. So, the MRI in all patients presenting with difficulty speaking is important 100% of the time.

The MRI also helps us tell if these patients have other illnesses. These same people can have multiple strokes, requiring different interventions. They can have focal infections, called abscesses. They can have inflammatory diseases, like multiple sclerosis or lupus. Finally, they can have aneurysms and tumors. You don't need to be a physician to realize the importance of these tests. In the past, when doctors only had the "clubs from 1930," they still figured out the correct diagnosis, eventually. Unfortunately, patients suffered with permanent disability and death while it took longer to figure out. They also went through risky tests, like brain biopsies, and many of them developed new problems from the tests themselves. Aren't you glad we can do this without puncturing the body or taking a piece of your brain out? Instead, we get the answer in 30 minutes instead of 3 weeks, or never?

Now is this cost effective? I doubt it. From a pure cost standpoint, if we forego the MRI and lose 1% of these people due to incorrectly diagnosing them as stroke when they had herpes encephalitis, we probably save a lot of money. That's what socialized medicine can give us because they look at a fixed number of dollars and allocate it to treat a population. They remove the individual patient from the equation.

Medical technology is an amazing thing. We can all agree that it is safer, quicker and allows us to diagnose and treat more effectively. Some Healthcare Reformers want you to believe that the only way to decrease healthcare costs is to limit tests. They do this under the guise that "doctors are ordering too many tests." So, they will limit the number of tests by limiting how many tests doctors can order. They focus on the more expensive tests, not taking into consideration the necessity of those tests. They aren't out there telling you, "we need to limit blood tests for liver function in patients taking cholesterol medications because the labs are almost always normal." They only focus on the MRI or cardiac catheterization because of their inherent cost. They do not waste time focusing on the true dollar spent and the true dollar saved because of these tests (as MRI's save lives and money also). Well, there are 2 ways to limit the costs of tests like MRI's. One is to limit the numbers, which is the only focus of the Healthcare Reformers. The other is to cut the cost of the tests. We could easily achieve the latter, still perform the needed tests, and still cut costs. It is Government regulations that limit the reduction of costs of MRI's. It we got rid of some restrictions on MRI's, made them more available, the cost would plummet. We could get the price down so most people could afford it out of their pocket and would not even need to charge the insurance company or Medicare. As we discussed, the demand is really not changeable. The demand is the need to use the MRI to help save or sustain your life. They want to control the demand, which will directly affect your health and life. THIS WILL COST LIVES AND MONEY! NO ONE CAN ARGUE AGAINST THAT POINT.

I do not want to focus on the economics of medicine. I again refer you to, "Who Killed Healthcare," by Regina Herzlinger for a true and in depth review. I just want to point out the absurd idea that we all will do better in healthcare by limiting technology and tests or access to physicians and specialists. We will not do better by limiting the very advancements that save our lives. You don't need to be a genius to realize that we need these tests to be more available, not less available, to save lives. That can only be done by making them cheaper. I promise, the Masters Tournament will not be more enjoyable with the professional golfers walking around with clubs from the 1930's, sans their putter, 7 iron, and driver.

By the way Tiger, even though we are giving you the 1930 technology and taking away your driver, 7 iron, and putter, we still expect a par or better on every hole. If it takes you too long to get to the hole, if you make an error with your swing with the rusty club along the way, or if you have a bogey on any hole, there will be a lawyer at the green ready for a lawsuit. You don't actually think the lawyers won't be able to sue doctors even though the Government takes away their technology and access to specialist referrals, do you? This is America. You can sue if you order hot coffee, drink it on purpose, and burn your mouth.

CHAPTER 7

The Players

In order to understand how the system works, I think it is vital to understand "the players" in the system. Not only do you need to understand who they are in 2009, you also need to understand how they got there, what motivates them, and you must understand their ultimate goals. As I write this, I have full expectations that some of the players will not only disappear (some added, some withdrawn), but their motivation and numbers will change.

Each health care participant has to answer to some authority. As one of my professors once said, despite his elevated status in the neurology department, "you are always somebody's boy."

The Patient: Well I am sorry to say that the consumer of health care, the patient, has no say in how health care works. They have no voice in policies, past or present, and will have no voice in the Healthcare Reformer's decision on how their health will be handled in the future. The patient was taken out of the decision process many years ago. Again, I will not go into too much detail as previous works (including those in my Bibliography) have all too painfully described how this all transpired. The consumer has only a few choices. The patient may see a list of benefits and lists of costs, or they may get to review nothing at all with a plan just handed to them. There is a list of the patient's responsibilities (or co-pays), but the patient has no idea of the true cost, as they are hidden and unavailable for review. The "co-pay" is also a largely made up number.

The patient has no voice in Washington, DC right now (nor did they ever). The patient wants a good price for a good product with health care, just as they do for everything else they purchase. Unfortunately, they do not have a "lobbyist" in DC to promote their requests or needs. They only hold a vote as a repercussion to remove a Government official. Cold hard cash to the politician's campaign probably works a lot better, which is why the big businesses in the game have lobbyists.

Who does the patient answer to? They only answer to the insurance company. Well, they certainly have friends and family who review the internet and weigh in on the situation (whether asked to give their opinion or not), but ultimately, the insurance company tells them what they can have. They often can't understand the complexities of their illnesses and rely on the physician's knowledge and experience. The physician can help them talk to the insurance company if they disagree with a limitation imposed by the company. This is sometimes easy, but often hard. However, there is at least always someone available at the insurance company for discussion.

The statistics of the "uninsured" patients are quite confusing right now. We have over 300 million people in the US. They tell us that about 45 million are uninsured. (That means that 255 million are insured.) Of the 45 million "uninsured", 10 million are expected to be non taxpaying illegal immigrants. 10 million are eligible for federal programs, but are not enrolled. 15 million have the money and ability to obtain insurance, but choose not to pay for it. (For instance, many young employed people don't feel the need to spend money on insurance they won't use.) That really leaves about 15 million people who can't find coverage. The individuals in the "uninsured group" do constantly change as their employment status changes. They are sick and lose insurance or they change jobs and lose insurance. Something definitely needs to be done for this group.

The Physician: I would like to say that things are better for the physician. The Government also removed us from the equation years ago. It is illegal for physicians to discuss costs of the care they provide with each other. Each one has no idea what the other is compensated for the same plan or procedure. The Government was concerned that physicians would band together and "price fix," so this became an anti-trust issue when Medicare was developed (i.e., when the Government officially became involved in your healthcare). This was a great win for the other players (besides the patients) as it allowed them to price-fix and deceive the patient and physician. The Physicians cannot decide to provide free or cheaper care. They are blinded to the true finances of healthcare, but bound to take what they are offered. Physicians apparently are not moral enough to handle a "conflict of interest" in healthcare. It's a good thing the malpractice attorneys, hospitals, insurance companies, and the pharmaceutical industry are moral enough to handle the conflict of interest they have in health care.

Physicians couldn't really fight this. The only real way would have been to go out on strike for their rights and those of the patients. The government and lobbyists knew that we couldn't all just go out on strike and let people die, right? So, we forged forward and complaints fell on deaf ears. No one would listen to a union of physicians that could pose little threat of strike. Doctors do not have a union anyway. There is an American Medical Association, but less than 25% of physicians are members. The AMA is not truly a union in that they do not fight much for doctors' rights and work conditions (hence the less than 25% participation).

Let me tell you about physicians. We worked very hard to become physicians. It is true, we did give up some of the best years of our lives, working un-Godly hours in college in order to get to Medical School. We didn't really mind doing this. In order to be good at our jobs and keep patients alive, we had to study a large volume of material and had to see thousands of patients to perfect our skills. Being a doctor is not about learning from a book. It is all about pattern recognition, bedside manner, and (for surgeons), technical skill. The more the exposure, the better the skill. Physicians understand that it is hard for someone to empathize with how hard we worked and we are not looking for sympathy. I have seen many movies about the Vietnam War. I have a general idea of what soldiers went through. However, I completely understand that I can't even conceive of what it is like to be in their shoes.

We are not completely altruistic, don't get me wrong. After all that work, and $200 thousand in debt, we hope to be compensated. We do want a good life and we want to be able to repay our financial debt. However, I never met a physician only "in it for the money." Quite frankly, we never catch up to most of our friends in business and our income is almost never the primary thing we worry about with health care reform.

The doctor's short term goal daily is to answer a particular patient's medical question. We want to figure out what needs to be done and how to treat the individual problem. We try to anticipate how this medical problem may cause other problems in the future. We would love to figure it out right way and never see that question come up again, i.e. fix the problem. We don't ever want to be wrong and, therefore, don't want calls or complaints telling us we got it wrong. We want to be able to answer the question with no tests at all. We would also love to answer the question with no medications or treatments. Obviously that isn't what happens most of the time and these questions require lifelong management in most cases.

That is really what the patient wants as well. They want to come to the office, tell us something, and have us do as few tests as possible to answer their question and fix it right away. They want that in ONE VISIT. The doctor and the patient want the same thing; their goals are aligned. The doctor, of course, wants to be paid a reasonable fee for this service, and I believe the patient wants to pay that reasonable fee. What "reasonable fee" means, of course, is unknown in 2009. That was easily answered years ago. One would think you could research "reasonable price" for anything under the sun in 2009 on the internet, but you can't with healthcare. (Again, far larger topic, covered only briefly in this book.) Doctors do naturally get upset by some inequities in payments in the medical system. Why does a spine surgeon make $400 thousand dollars per year, while the salesman who distributes the screws used by the surgeon makes $1 million dollars per year? This seems unfair given the fact that the patient's life is in the hands of the surgeon while the salesman has no risk or liability.

Physicians do answer to higher authorities. If one is an academic physician, there are department heads above them, who in turn, have to answer to hospital and medical school administrations. But, the academic physician really responds to the Department Chairperson, and their work has to justify their continued employment.

In private practice or private hospital, where most physicians work in 2009, each physician answers to their group or hospital administrator. There are hundreds of different set-ups in private practice, but the hierarchy is usually pretty simple. Income is based on performance and performance is based on predetermined measure. If you work for a hospital, you are usually paid a salary.

All physicians, however, answer to insurance companies. No matter what we think is the best test or treatment plan, ultimately, this needs to be approved by an insurance company. Most of this is predetermined. We order tests and treatments that are already approved. Sometimes we have to make extra calls to justify our plan with the company. Some care is done "out of pocket," but most is done within the guidelines of the insurance plan. If the doctor really disagrees with the company, there are guidelines for appealing insurance company decisions. Sometimes this is easy, often it is hard and takes an inappropriate amount of time.

A doctor's biggest problem in 2009 is paperwork and the time it adds. We spend more time on paperwork than we do with patients in many cases. We have more overhead and employee positions to do paperwork, pre-certifications and interactions with insurance companies. We need to generate enough revenue to pay for all of this. The paperwork adds so much time and financial strain on the system that the provider has to spend less time with patients.

The Hospital: One would assume that the hospital's only goal is to provide the best care possible to patients. It's simple right? You hire the best doctors and have the best facility, the best care is sure to follow. When you provide the best care, patients will flock to your hospital and everyone is happy.

However, there are so many factors involved, so many rules and regulations, so many different types of patients, and so many Boards and insurance companies, that this is too simplistic. Hospitals take care of patients that are located near their doors. So, if there is a lot of trauma in the area, as in many inner cities, the hospital gets a lot of patients with gunshot wounds and bodily injury. These types of patients are more likely to be uninsured. If the hospital is in an area where general medical care is sparse (again in the inner city or in a very rural community), patients are often very sick when they present to the hospital. Some hospitals are in areas where insured patients are plentiful, while others are in areas with many uninsured patients.

Because of this, many years ago with some good insight, the government figured out they would need some regulations to benefit hospitals that take care of people who can't pay. Otherwise, these facilities would not be able to stay open. As usual, however, with excellent lobbying from the hospital associations, these regulations blossomed and further benefited hospitals that didn't need help. The system allowed abuse, which further perpetuated the health care problem, and raised costs.

The hospital does at least provide a necessary service to the patient. However, their bottom line is financial. The hospital is run by a Board. The Board is completely detached from the patient, the doctor and the nurses. They look at things much like the CEO and Board at IBM look at their business. Yes, we need to provide a service and we need to compete with APPLE, but they are focused on the $ sign at the end of the year. They will not support efforts that will lose money, even if they help the patient. True, they do support some "money losers" as part of the hospital process, but do so only if it helps bring in other money, such as by bringing more patients to their facility for higher paying procedures.

The hospital also has to interact with the insurance industry. This is probably the biggest battle in health care. They are at odds with each other, and one loses often when the other gains. They each have the strongest lobbies in Washington, DC. Is it a surprise then that the Government regulations in health care benefit those 2 groups and not the patient and physician?

The Insurance Industry: Ok. So I tried to come up with a benefit that the insurance company provides the patient. I failed! The insurance industry is a business. They are not the friend of the patient, nor do they provide any physical service that improves patient's lives or longevity. In the end, they want to amass the largest sum of money by year's end to make the board of directors and stockholders happy. Let's face it, they make more money by withholding care and medicines from the patient. Don't get me wrong, this is not an easy task and does have risk. They do not have a large profit margin and they run the risk of losing money. I am all for the free market, but not when it is unfair and at the expense of the patient.

There is a certain amount of money that comes into the insurance company each year based on how many patients sign up. At the end of the year, the profit is simply the number of patients paying into the plan minus the money spent on the care of those patients. The less they pay for the doctors, tests, hospitals, and medications, the happier the Board and the more they pay out to the executives in bonuses. (A CEO of an insurance company can make $50-100 million in a bonus). If they want to make more money the next year, they only have 2 options. One, they can pay even less to the doctors, for tests, the hospitals, and to pharmacies. Two, they can charge the patients more. The Insurance company actually does both to raise profits. They also get rid of the "sick people" as they spend more on sicker patients. They make a greater profit by increasing the price of the plan to the healthy people, who don't need tests or doctors very often, and get rid of sicker people.

Again, this is a topic that would take volumes to discuss. Why the Government has not only allowed this to happen, but has supported legislation that promotes it, is deplorable. Does it have anything to do with the $ millions spent in Washington, DC by the lobbyists?

(My heart is racing and my blood is boiling as I write this. I have been listening to politicians in 2009 blame everyone else but themselves for the healthcare crises they created. They are telling us that they, the US Government, will fix the problem when they had the devilish hand in the process. They are using words like "Medicare Fraud" that are mostly deceptive to make the doctors and hospitals look like criminals. Their regulations allowed the costs to rise. The insurance companies really haven't done anything "wrong"; they have played within the rules developed by the politicians in Washington, D.C.)

The insurance industry, in essence, is the only player that really has no alliance with the consumer. They win when the patient stays healthy on their own, or when the company withholds care. Very simply, they are at odds with the consumer's best interest.

My only defense of the Health Insurance Industry is that they are bound by Government regulations. These regulations, in the end, prevent costs from going down. They are not performing on an equal playing field and they have done nothing illegal. If the Federal Government would make things more transparent and lift many insurance regulations, the companies would be able to compete nationally. This competition would bring costs down as they would be forced to compete for your insurance dollars.

The Pharmaceutical Industry: Like the Insurance Industry, the pharmaceutical industry exists as a business. They need to provide profits for Boards, executives and stock holders. They do this by charging as much as possible for a drug.

However, they do provide a service vital to patient survival. Without medications, we don't live very long. They started prolonging our lives with the advent of antibiotics. They make the most money if they not only have a drug that works, but also has very few side effects. This is 100% in line with what the patient wants: a cure for the illness with a drug that causes NO problems.

This not an easy thing to accomplish, nor is it cheap. It costs roughly $500-800 million dollars to bring a drug to market. They study more than 10 drugs that fail for every one that makes it to market. For each additional indication for a specific drug, it costs another $30-50 million. So, if they want the FDA to allow them to promote their drug and get insurance coverage for another indication, even if science has already studied the indication and it's accepted in the medical community by experts, it still costs them an additional $30-50 million. Neurontin (gabapentin) is an example. Neurontin was approved by the FDA for seizures. It turned out to be a well tolerated, safe medication for the treatment of nerve related pain. Many studies by academic centers showed how effective and safe the drug was for nerve related pain. However, if they wanted to include nerve related pain as an official

FDA approved indication, it would have cost an additional $30-50 million for more FDA approved studies.

Summary: What I have tried to do in this chapter is give a very brief description of the players and their roles in the health care system in 2009. This will change and I suspect, therefore, that the health care game will change. I wanted the reader to try to look at health care in 2009 versus the future, and understand the 2009 motives for the doctors, hospitals and the insurance industry. I suspect that the doctors and patients will be further marginalized in the future and the industries with expensive lobbies will do just fine.

The patient's motive in health care will not change. They want the best health care for a reasonable price in order to live a long, prosperous, and pain free life. They want this service to be all inclusive and they want it to be convenient, i.e. not to intrude much on their valuable time. Our system is too expensive, but it is far more encompassing and far more efficient than government run systems that exist here in the US or in other countries. With a few Government regulatory changes, the expenses would go down.

I do not suspect that the motives for doctors will change. As stated, we want also to provide comprehensive care in a pain free, expedient manner. Our abilities and rules will change, but not our motives. We want fair reimbursement for our work and preparation (college, pre-medical and medical school studies, and years of residency). Reimbursement is not the main objective for physicians, however. If there is not fair reimbursement, then the training and types of people who go into the field will suffer. Hence, patient care will suffer. If there is not fair reimbursement, the Government will have to take on the task of educating the doctors. Remember, that's about 18,000 students a year at the tune of $200-350,000 per student. That does not include the expense of paying the medical schools, doctors and teaching hospitals. Ultimately, that cost will fall on the taxpayer.

The real question is how the motives of insurance companies and hospitals will change under the new health care system. How well will their lobbies protect their interests and how much power will the government take away from them? We shall see.

It will be most interesting to see what happens to the pharmaceutical industry. While they are "no angels," they are also not the BEAST the media portrays them to be in 2009. Remember, they provide a service that you and I need to survive. The best doctor or hospital in the world won't be successful at helping people in the future with current "incurable diseases" without the drug companies. They are a business and need some incentive to spend $300 million to develop a new drug. They provide a service that the consumer desperately needs and wants.

At this point, those who know me are wondering why I haven't gone into medical malpractice as a player in the system? Well, I could spend months writing on this topic and write about how this costs all patients, the government, and taxpayers billions of unnecessary dollars a year. I leave it out because Congress is made up of lawyers, the Trial Lawyers Association has the biggest lobby effort of all in DC, so I have little reason to believe health care reform will change the way we worry about malpractice. I assure you of only 1 thing. The day I am forced to follow Government protocols in patient decisions and I am still liable for malpractice despite following the protocol, I will cease to practice medicine. We'll see if that happens, but it appears this will be the case based on recent comments of the President to the American Medical Association. It seems that he believes that we can have physicians follow protocols and this will limit malpractice claims. The problem with that concept is that medicine does not follow rigid protocols and a patient's status changes at variable rates. Every patient is different. The legal system has all the advantages. A lawsuit can arise when no error is made (as is statistically the case in 80% of all malpractice claims reviewed). A protocol will not change this and I suspect malpractice will flourish in the next 10 years. In my opinion, the reform ideas I have read thus far will actually help malpractice attorneys. I don't really think the Government is out to increase malpractice in the US, but who knows. Maybe Healthcare Reform should be renamed "The Malpractice Attorney Stimulus Package of 2009."

I do recommend that the people in New York and California look at moving to the South and Midwest. Those 2 States have some of the highest malpractice insurance costs. What happens when a doctor's income is greatly reduced? How is he going to afford malpractice insurance (which I predict will go up, not down in the first decade of the new health system)? Right now, the salary pays for the malpractice (it is a business cost). When the revenue goes down, doctors will first let a lot of employees go, but will eventually be forced to stop practicing in some states. In these States, we may find doctors only in hospitals where malpractice is covered by the institution. Some surgical specialties (like neurosurgery) have malpractice premiums in the $150,000/year range. I predict many of them will be forced to move to States where medical malpractice is better handled, currently States in the South and Midwest.

Chapter 8

How a Doctor Thinks

Everyone needs to understand how physicians are trained to take care of patients. Sometimes, things are quite simple. For example, if your blood pressure is up, we know the long term complications and we recommend treatment with either exercise, stress management or medications. If you have strep throat, we understand the implications of antibiotics versus complications of untreated strep throat, so we offer antibiotics.

We don't always know what is going on and often have to order tests to figure it out. We also order tests to monitor therapies. When it comes to tests, we ask ourselves 2 things in order to decide if tests are needed:

1. Will the test tell me something that I do not know? There is no reason to order a test if we already know the answer.

2. Once I get the information from the test, will it change the way I treat this patient? If not, then why do I need the test and why would I want the information? For instance, if a 95 year old female comes to me and I think she has compression on her spinal cord in the neck, I could order an MRI of her cervical spine to confirm that suspicion. However, if this person is not a surgical candidate, as she has metastatic cancer and has requested

no further medical intervention, then there is no reason to order the test.

Obviously, we don't know ahead of time if these tests will be abnormal or not. Advocates of health care reform always talk about "unnecessary tests." Well, they consider all negative tests "unnecessary" when they tell you how much money is wasted. They don't factor in that most of these tests are indicated, i.e. done for the right reason, but they are often negative. Just because a test is normal, which is great for the patient, doesn't mean it was unnecessary! When I do a brain MRI suspecting a tumor, I am always happy when a test comes back negative. When a cardiologist believes a patient has life threatening cardiovascular disease, he or she is always happy to see the tests come back negative. This does not mean those tests were "unnecessary," it just means that it is very often difficult to tell what is going on before doing some tests. If medicine was that easy, medical school would be 1 year instead of 4 and there would be very little need for an extra 3-7 years of post medical school training.

Now, I am not naive, I fully understand that some doctors probably order unnecessary tests in order to pad their pockets financially. However, this is an exception and not the norm. This is having little to no impact on the overall health care costs. Trust me, there was not a single class in medical school, or a single course in residency, that discussed the business of medicine. That's why physicians are thought of as bad businesspeople.

There is a final caveat in how and when we decide to order tests. Once we know we need to order a test that will change the way we treat someone, we have to decide how quickly this needs to be done. Is it emergent and we need to send the patient right to the emergency room? Can this be done in the next week or so (meaning it's urgent but not emergent)? Is it something we can delay? (For example, if you have signs of carpal tunnel syndrome, but your exam looks pretty good, we can follow a slower course of action. We can go ahead and use some splints at night, for $10, instead of ordering a test that might cost $500. There is no harm in waiting and watching as it will not hurt you in the long run.)

This is the part of health care reform that concerns most physicians, especially in a litigious society. We are trained to know how concerning your symptoms are and what might happen if our suspicion is correct. You don't learn this in medical school or from a text book. It takes years of post medical school training, a huge volume of patients with similar symptoms, to understand what is urgent or emergent. Physicians are most concerned that limiting tests may, for example, delay a cardiac catheterization and may cause death in someone who could have been saved. We are concerned that delaying an MRI of the neck or low back, for example, could lead to disabling paraplegia or weakness in a young and healthy productive mother of 4.

We are also very afraid of what the lawyers will do to us. Even if we know a patient needs a test and we know how urgently one needs to be done, health care rationing may delay this process or exclude it entirely. Just because we know what to do and recommended it be done quickly, in a court of law in the USA, we are held responsible if it does not get done. In Great Britain, a doctor is not sued if he follows the protocol, no matter what happens. If you think I am paranoid, I can tell you this happens now. If a doctor orders a test immediately and the patient decides not to get it done, the doctor is responsible if there is a bad outcome that could have been prevented had the patient gone for the test. For instance, if a doctor tells a patient to go right to the emergency room for a cardiac catheterization, the patient is rolled to the ER in a wheelchair by that MD, and then the patient gets up and leaves the hospital and dies of a massive heart attack, the family can still sue that doctor. I can always convince an insurance company to allow a test I feel necessary. It just takes a phone call. Do you think the Federal Government will be so flexible and communicative?

CHAPTER 9

The Physician's Practice: 2009

Strep Throat/Tonsillectomy

Since President Obama started me on this voyage with his strep throat example, I decided to elaborate on his further. I rarely treat strep throat anymore and am not an expert, but I think I still know enough to teach everyone why a child ever gets a tonsillectomy. I take on a primary care role in many of my patients with multiple sclerosis, so I do treat strep throat on occasion.

Remember, a tonsillectomy is performed by an Ear, Nose, and Throat Surgeon, not a pediatrician. The pediatrician makes NO MONEY when he refers a patient for this procedure and is therefore doing it in the best interest of the patient. The ENT doctor does not comb the halls of pediatrician's offices looking for tonsils to remove. When a patient is referred into their office for evaluation of the procedure, the physician reviews the patient's history and examines the patient. If he or she agrees that the indications are correct, the surgeon discusses the pros and cons of the tonsillectomy in an open discussion with the family.

Strep throat is very common. Everyone reading this book has had it, likely many times. When you have a sore throat accompanied by other symptoms, strep (a bacteria) is the likely cause. Those symptoms are fever, pus in the tonsils, swollen lymph nodes and the absence of cough. Cough often suggests a virus instead of a bacteria, which does not need antibiotics. Well, when a child presents with a sore throat, they usually have some of these findings and symptoms, but not all. One does not want to treat a virus, but antibiotics can be life saving if it is the strep bacteria. Untreated strep throat can lead to cardiac complications (rheumatic fever), kidney failure, and death. I see adult patients who have had strokes or kidney failure from the strep bacteria as a child.

It is now generally accepted that when a child has strep throat more than 2-3 times in a year, a tonsillectomy should be considered. Strep throat is uncomfortable, gets kids out of school and parents out of work, and requires frequent antibiotics. I have already told you the complications of strep throat, but you must also realize that frequent use of antibiotics is also a concern. As we have all heard, there is a small pandemic with patients carrying antibiotic resistant bacteria. Frequent use of antibiotics is the major cause. How does the tonsillectomy help the patient? Well, it seems that these children, with frequent strep throat, essentially become "carriers" of the bacteria in the tonsils. By removing them, they greatly reduce the frequency, and therefore, risks of further strep throat. The risks of cardiac and kidney disease go down. The risk of developing a resistance to antibiotics goes down.

Pediatricians actually would make "more money" by allowing the kids to keep coming into the office, charging a co-pay, billing the insurance company and running the rapid strep test at every office encounter. They refer to the ENT physician when the clinical situation suggests the child would do better with a tonsillectomy. The ENT surgeon does not pay the pediatrician for the referral, send him a restaurant gift card, or take him or her out to play golf. The referral and surgery are done in the patient's best interest.

Concerns for the future: Who will decide the criteria for tonsillectomies? When the criteria are still met, how long will it take to get the surgery done? If the criteria doesn't change, 2-3 strep throats in a year gets you an ENT referral, how long will it take to see the actual doctor and how long will it take to schedule the procedure in a medical center? Remember, socialized medicine is as much about delaying care (or payments) as it is about limiting care. My daughter got her tonsillectomy about 3 weeks after it was suggested by the pediatrician, which included ENT referral and evaluation. Delaying the surgery could lead to one of the aforementioned complications or even death. Delaying the surgery means more days the parent has to stay home from work and the child misses school. Delay and more antibiotics increase the likelihood of developing resistance to antibiotics.

But Wait, There's More

Let's stick with inaccuracies suggested by the Healthcare Reformers. Politician's speeches are truly the "gift that keeps on giving" if you listen to what they are really saying and you have a good sense of humor. President Obama is a politician, so he is no different. In August, 2009, he did a town hall meeting in New Hampshire to push the health care reform process. He was talking about the treatment of people with diabetes and their primary care physician. Now, I am not an eloquent politician, but I will tell you at least how I interpreted this example he used as he was trying to point out the problems with health care today.

He stated that there were "no incentives" for primary care physicians to take good care of patients with diabetes. Forget the education and dedication the primary care physician has for all his or her patients. The President said because they were paid a mere "5 pence" to take care of these patients, they didn't spend the time needed to adequately take care of their diabetic patients. If they were paid more, they would work harder and work on the patient's diet, their lifestyle, and there would be better outcomes. If they were paid more, the costs of diabetic care would go down. He inferred that the greedy doctors just needed a little more financial incentive to do the right thing and take better care of the patient.

Well, I tell you, if I was a primary care physician, that set of statements would have sent me over the edge. The President was telling the American people that these doctors give sub-optimal care because they are not paid enough. Because of under payment, the physician's neglect leads to expensive surgeries. After years of education and personal sacrifice, after countless hours dedicated to diabetic patients teaching them the best way to manage their disease, after countless hours educating patients on how to live longer with better diabetes control, the President was insinuating that these doctors do a bad job because they are not paid enough. He implied that the complications of diabetes were the fault of the physician.

Let's look at this a bit closer. The Healthcare Reformers want everyone to believe that patients are all alike. If we just give them the correct medications, talk about prevention, everyone will do just fine. This, unfortunately, is completely false. What makes a doctor's job so difficult and so interesting is that no 2 patients are alike. No 2 patients respond to medications the same. Unfortunately, this also defies the truth about human nature as well. No 2 patients, given all the tools needed to control their diabetes, will follow the regimen the same. They will not eat the right foods in the same amount, they will "fall off the wagon" differently, they will exercise differently, and they will adhere to the best advice differently.

Let's even go crazy here and step into a fantasy world for a second. Let's say we have an artificial pancreas device that can be planted under every patient's skin. For fantasy sake, let's say the artificial pancreas device is free and has no complications. It works exactly the same in every patient. Every patient who has this device is hand delivered the same food and is transported daily to do the same required exercise program. They can't go into a fast food restaurant because the device sets off an alarm and they are redirected by the "Pancreas Police." All of these fantasy patients have no other medical problems and they are promised that none will ever develop as long as they have this "magical artificial pancreas." Well, dear Reformers, even then all of the patients will develop complications of diabetes and will do so in a different manner and timeframe. Even then, oh wise Reformers, some will lose their toes, ankles and legs. Some will still develop blindness and lose their nerves and kidneys. Yes, some will even still have heart attacks and strokes. I believe also that some may die eventually, and will do so at different times.

It does not matter what you pay the primary care physician, many patients will not listen and many patients will still need the surgeon. In fact, all of them will still develop complications of diabetes. In the real world, the human body is an amazing machine that handles disease differently and will break and eventually die. Even in fantasy land, people get sick and die and there's nothing you can do about that fact.

In the President's example, he stated that the primary care physician got paid a mere "5 pence" while the surgeon was paid "$30,000" to perform the amputation. Let's look at the facts and truth a little more closely. For a foot amputation, the hospital bill probably comes out to about $30,000. The vascular surgeons wish they were paid even 25% of that bill. The actual amount they are paid is approximately $900 by Medicare. That includes the entire procedure, with all its risks, and subsequent visits related to the procedure. This probable amounts to about $50/hour. When a cardiovascular surgeon performs and open heart surgery, they are paid about $2500, while the hospital makes $40-50,000. The surgeon takes on all the risk and needs all the skill, yet they are paid a mere fraction of what the hospital is paid. They make the same amount, by the way, regardless of how long the patient is in the hospital or how many complications arise.

For further analysis, let's say this patient's primary care physician helped them with their diabetes for 10 years. Let's say the patient came in 4 times a year. If the primary care physician was paid $40 per visit, he or she actually made $1,200 over those 10 years. The surgeon made $900. So, how is it that the Presidents "5 pence" example is in any way correct? You guessed it, it's not. Either the example was a lie or he was misinformed.

It is also true that there has never been a study truly showing that "preventative medicine" spread over the entire US population will save money. **The fact is that numerous studies have proven that preventative medicine, including screening tests, greatly increases the cost of health care**. Individually, in certain patients, preventative interventions save money. If you take a specific diabetic (since we're on the subject) and put them in a diet and exercise program, you can extend their life. If this was free to everyone with diabetes, then you could extend lives in many, but not all diabetics. As with my insulin fantasy device story, all the diabetic patients will still die and the complications you are trying to avoid will still happen in most patients. Some complications may be delayed, but they will still come. We are not in fantasy land (well at least most aren't anyway) and the preventative measures will cost money. The education will still cost money. The patients will still not be 100% compliant with their diet and exercise. The cost of the preventative measures will exceed what you would have spent otherwise because it will be spread among a far greater # of people than will benefit. For example, if you spend $10,000 on five patients with a complication, that will cost $50,000. That is far less than if you spend $1 on 100,000 diabetic patients with prevention, as that will cost $100,000. This is not only common sense, but is statistically true. It may not be politically favorable, but it is true.

Let's further examine the "butcher" or surgeon who is just waiting to cut the patient's foot off. Well, this "butcher" also trained for many long years and made many sacrifices in his or her personal life. As a matter of fact, every one of them trained many more years than the primary care physician and their training was harder and more rigorous than any primary care physician. (No offense to the primary care physicians is intended. My training is much more similar to the primary care physician than the surgeon.) They did 2 years of grueling internships (first a medical then a surgical). They then did a surgical residency and most "butchers of the diabetic foot" did extra training to become a vascular specialist. Their daily life is much harder as well. Most of them go to the hospital around 5 am daily to see their hospital patients, followed by a full day in the office or operating room, culminating in rounding in the hospital at night.

When the patient comes in to see the primary care physician, there is little or no chance that the patient is going to die during that office visit. There is an extremely low likelihood that anything is going to go wrong. The patient will walk out of that encounter no worse off than when they came in. The same cannot be said for the surgical encounter. Let me tell you a few truths about the risks of an amputation surgery. During and soon after the surgery, the patient has a risk of dying. There is a risk of the heart stopping when placed under anesthesia. There is a risk of a blood clot forming in the limb which can travel to the lungs or heart causing death. There is a risk of infection in the limb, which can lead to more surgeries or death if it spreads. After surgery, the risk of infection continues and other complications arise that can also lead to death. The surgeon is trained very well to avoid these complications, hence the extra years of training and all the added sleepless nights.

By the way, do you realize that all of the complications noted above with the surgery are much, much, much more likely in a diabetic patient? Do you realize that a diabetic patient with vascular disease requiring surgery also has other blood vessels in the body? I don't know if the Healthcare Reformers are aware, but the heart, kidneys, and brain also have blood vessels. I don't know if they are aware that the skin, intestines, and all other tissues of the body have the same blood vessels. If we can teach them that, then maybe they can understand that when a foot has no blood supply due to diabetes, there's a 100% chance that other organs have a problem with their blood vessels also to some degree. The surgeon has no idea how bad and which organs are the worst. But, the surgeon is aware that any one of those organs could shut down due to vascular disease at anytime during and after the surgery. Hence, the risk is much higher in a diabetic patient with vascular disease.

Now remember, I am a neurologist. I am much more like the primary care physician than the surgeon. I would love it if I was paid as much as a neurosurgeon, but I understand that I don't deserve to be. I follow patients for years for conditions, such as brain tumors and cervical disc disease. I am well aware that when the neurosurgeon is needed to help my patients, as these conditions worsen, they will get paid far more for the surgery. I don't mind at all that they get paid for their expertise in managing a highly risky process to help my patients. I understand that it's risky to open up a skull or a spine, to operate on brain or spine. I understand that surrounding those tissues are a whole lot of blood vessels that can rupture and cause immediate death. I understand that despite studying anatomy and doing operations for years, everybody is different and each person's anatomy is different. So, each surgery is actually different. We train these neurosurgeons for years to learn how to handle this extra risk which takes extra skill. I am alright with the concept that we pay some people more than we pay the primary care physician or the medical neurologist.

By the way, the primary care physician and the neurologist do not make any more money for the referral to the vascular surgeon or neurosurgeon. We do the referral because it's in the best interest of our patients.

Concerns for the future: I do not believe that any of the cost savings suggested will actually reduce costs in the future US healthcare system. Preventative medicine is an example noted above. When the cost savings don't exist, where will they go for the money to cover everyone? Well, as in Great Britain or Canada, they will go to rationing. They will also go to raising taxes. In the end, we again won't save more people or extend lives. We will simply pick ahead of time, who will die. For those of you who say we already do that, as the poor or unemployed have no money for insurance, I disagree. 100% of the US population can get care by going into an Emergency Room in the US, regardless of age or insurance.

Warning to the Healthcare Reformers:

CIGARETTE SMOKING IS ANOTHER INDEPENDENT MAJOR RISK FACTOR FOR PERIPHERAL VASCULAR DISEASE. PEOPLE WHO SMOKE ARE MORE LIKELY TO NEED THE "BUTCHER" TO CUT HIS OR HER FOOT OFF AT SOME POINT IN THEIR FUTURE. SO IF ANY OF YOU HEALTHCARE REFORMERS KNOW ANYONE IN WASHINGTON, D.C. WHO HAS A PROBLEM WITH SMOKING, YOU MIGHT WANT TO PASS ALONG THAT TIDBIT OF INFORMATION (AND MAYBE THE PHONE NUMBER OF A VASCULAR SURGEON)!

The Truth About Economics in a Physicians Practice

I have never once thought about money when I made a decision or recommendation for a patient. Let me repeat that: I HAVE NEVER ONCE THOUGHT ABOUT MONEY WHEN I MADE A DECISION OR RECOMMENDATION FOR A PATIENT. Ironically, although doctors are very well educated and intelligent, in general they are terrible businessmen and businesswoman. There is not a single class in medical school on medical economics. There is not a single class in medical school on running a medical practice. Finally, there is not a single class in medical school that discusses how to use tests and procedures to benefit a doctor's bank account.

We have 3 offices, 8 physicians, and about 80 employees. Over 80 percent of those employees have families that are covered under the health insurance we provide. Most are not covered by their spouses (for those who are married). We have set up a Pension and Profit Sharing, or 401K, Program to enable our employees to save for their retirement. 100% of them contribute. Since we are technically a "small business," the contributions to the plans come out of our revenue stream and, at the end of the year, out of the physician's pockets.

If we let our business fail, all of this goes away. We depend on a great staff to provide efficient and excellent care. Because of this, we are well respected throughout our State and region. We even have patients who drive from the 4 surrounding States to come to our offices. If we provide subpar care, our reputation is injured, we see less patients, and our revenue decreases. If our staff is subpar, they anger patients and our revenue goes down with the decrease in patient referrals. We need to make sure that our care is exemplary, our staff is exemplary, and our patients get the best of care.

On a day to day basis, even a month to month basis, we do not review "pay scales" or the revenue generated by the things we do. You need to understand medical economics to understand this. Fee scales for procedures, drugs, examinations, etc... change on a constant basis. When Medicare makes an adjustment on a drug or procedure, it may be 6-12 months for insurers to change accordingly. When a drug company changes the cost of a medication we provide in our office, it may be 6-12 months before all of the insurance carriers or Medicare adjust their reimbursement. (Of course, they usually raise the price of the drug and it may be a long time before the reimbursement goes up the same amount, if ever.) Since the Government has set up so many regulations that limit communication about prices or reimbursement to physicians and hospitals (i.e. anti-trust regulations), no one physician has any idea if their pay scale from an insurance company is above or below other physicians or institutions. When pay scales change for us, they may be unaffected for other physicians, and we have no way of knowing. This is in no way based on excellence of care and is completely arbitrary, often at the discretion of the insurance company. My point is that there are too many arbitrary, ever changing factors in reimbursement. It is impractical to monitor these factors on a day to day basis.

As I stated, I have 80 employees, plus their families, that depend on my work and reputation for their well being. It would be improper for me to ignore the business of my practice and let it go bankrupt. We therefore need to analyze our practice in a business manner in order to make sure we keep the doors open. We do this on a yearly basis essentially, with some evaluation every 6 months. If a service we provide causes us to lose money, we have to do one of 2 things. We either figure out a way to provide it elsewhere, or we eat the costs. Often we just eat the costs as long as it doesn't cause us to go bankrupt. Often, we find a site to provide the service, as many services are reimbursed better at an institution, like a hospital. For instance, it costs about $300 to do an MRI on our MS patients. MRI's are crucial to monitor their disease progression and response to treatments. When one insurance company reduced our MRI reimbursement to $200/patient, we started doing their MRI's at a local hospital. Hospitals get far greater reimbursement on MRI's, so they were happy to take on 10% of our patient's MRI's. (Our MRI reimbursement varies from $450 per patient to $850 per patient. Most hospitals get reimbursed $1500-2500 per MRI. Ironically, by shifting MRI's over to the hospital from our office, the insurance company essentially raised their cost on MRI's.)

When we shift a procedure over to another institution, it still costs us money. We still need to hire an employee to pre-certify the procedure. We still need someone to set up the study and track the results. So, we lose money, but we lose less money. Why do we do this? Because we feel it's a service or procedure that is in the best interest of the patient (another great example of how we serve our patients, not our bank accounts).

Now, there is only so much revenue neutral or revenue negative care we can provide. At the end of the day, we need to be able to pay for our employees and rent, or the business shuts down. We do the yearly analysis to decide where we need to limit our losses. WE DO NOT LOOK AT THE REVENUE GAIN OR LOSS ON A DAILY BASIS, MUCH LESS ON AN INDIVIDUAL PATIENT BASIS, AS WAS SUGGESTED ON WEDNESDAY, JULY 22, 2009! We do, however, analyze costs and revenue on a quarterly and yearly basis in order to ensure our practice stays open and we are able to provide what we feel are necessary services for our patients. Unlike many businesses, we continue to provide care that causes us to lose money, because it is in the best interest of the patient.

As mentioned before, I guarantee more than 90% of physicians would be glad to see patients for free if the rules were changed. The hospitals get huge tax breaks for free care. Not only does the physician not get a tax break, it is also illegal as it violates Medicare rules. (Yes, it violates the rules set up by the Government.) I guarantee if the government gave doctors 1/2 the tax break the hospital sees for free care of the uninsured, most doctors would gladly see patients for free. Heck, I bet most doctors would actually advertise and compete for these free patients! Doctors being incentivized to see patients for free; seems too simple so I doubt they have considered this in Washington, D.C.

There are a few other interesting general statistics about a physician's office. If a physician works 5 days a week, the first 3 days pay for overhead. They generate revenue only on the latter 2 days. They actually don't generate pure income on those 2 days because when they go on vacation, the office still works and they are not generating revenue. Therefore, most physicians get paid for 1.5 days out of their 5 day work week. Also, a very well run practice will have 55-60% overhead. If the office is not well run, this number is higher. Physicians are not trained businessmen and businesswomen, so many offices are not well run and their overhead is much higher. With these statistics, it's easy to see that a physician can't offer many services that lose money if they want to be able to pay for their staff, rent, and still have income at the end of the year.

There's another malpractice irony here worth mentioning. I will use myself as an example, but you can extrapolate this to any doctor who orders any test if they have been even remotely trained to review that test. This example includes primary care physicians who look at chest X-Rays or orthopedic surgeons who review knee MRI's. I have been trained to look at MRI's of brain and spinal cord. In fact, I have seen more than most radiologists that specialize in MRI's of brain and spinal cord. Even if a radiologist gets paid to perform the MRI and reads the MRI, I am still responsible legally to interpret the MRI correctly. In order to do so, I have to spend the time to look at the MRI and interpret it correctly. If the radiologist reads it wrong, I am still the one responsible, so I must spend the time to look at it myself.

Kind of ironic, isn't it? The Reformers do not want me to be paid for doing the MRI, but they still want me to be liable.

Efficiency of Care

As mentioned in a previous chapter, all doctors are trained to take a patient's history, do an exam, and, through years of experience, learn how to figure out if there are any warning signs of imminent trouble. If nothing concerning pops up, we watch. If something obvious and easy to treat pops up, we treat it. You can imagine when doctors see 20-30 patients a day, with such a large number of people in the USA, very often signs of medical urgencies and emergencies come up. When there are emergencies, we get patients right to the hospital (no matter what the insurance situation). Very often there are life threatening or life altering signs outside of our particular area of expertise. I am trained in neurology. Most medical students have 4 weeks of neurology experience. Some medical students have no neurology experience. In residency and fellowship, I gained 4 more years of neurology experience. I have now added 9 extra years of experience in private practice. I have seen thousands of patients with particular neurological symptoms, where the primary care physician may have seen these symptoms once or not at all.

Most primary care physicians can pick up a neurological emergency as these are often dramatic. For example, if a patient suddenly can't walk or talk, this is an obvious emergency. These people go right to the hospital. However, often a neurological condition that is life threatening can be hard to diagnose and is much more subtle. In our current system, it is quite simple to get an expert opinion on a patient's condition and do so rather quickly. My group gets about 8 calls a day from physicians who have questions about a patient. Over the phone, we decide if the patient needs to be seen in our office or the hospital, and how quickly. Often, the patient does not need to be seen at all. My office visit and an outpatient evaluation is thousands of dollars cheaper than the hospital, so these phone calls save money. Often, the symptom is benign and does not need any further work-up or treatment, which obviously saves the system the most money. I know if something needs to be done because I have seen it a thousand times. If the primary care physician no longer has access to a specialist or a referral, they will be much more inclined to just order unnecessary tests or admit people unnecessarily to the hospital. That is simple and understandable. How can a physician be expected to handle things properly when they have not been adequately trained to do so? One cannot learn these skills from a book, but by experience only. The more one sees, the better they become.

As a specialist, we have an unwritten rule. We want to make sure that a routine referral to our practice takes no longer than 2-3 weeks. We understand that we will lose patients if the referral takes longer. The patient will look elsewhere. Let's think about this and compare it to Great Britain. It should take no more than 2-3 weeks to see most specialists in the US. Sometimes, when things are busy or if we are in short supply, it may take 4-6 weeks. In Great Britain, if you can get a referral to a specialist, it can take OVER 4-6 MONTHS. If you are a young person who can't talk correctly or move your arm all of a sudden, you have a high chance of being dead or disabled in a month, much less 6 months. It is not normal to develop difficulty moving an arm, or difficulty walking, or difficulty speaking. These are not conditions that should be addressed over months, but minutes, days, or weeks. If a patient needs to be seen quickly and the waiting list is over 2-3 weeks, the patient most often still gets seen quickly without going to the hospital. If a referring physician calls the specialist, the patient gets in right away. In my practice, I see overbooked patients about 4-5 times a week. I see them on my lunch hour, I extend my day, or I see them at 7 a.m. before my clinic starts. I do so because it's the right thing to do for the patient and for the physician who is asking for my expertise as they know it is beyond their training.

This efficiency and convenience for patients is not free either. In our 3 offices, we have 4-5 employees working at any one time taking care of non-reimbursable needs for our patients. We have people answering phone calls with patient concerns or symptoms. We have people calling in refills for prescriptions. We have 4 full time positions working on pre-certification of tests to get them approved by the insurance companies so patients will not have to pay out of their pockets. Most of the tests we order are done outside of our office and we gain no revenue from the tests. Finally, we have these same people filling out forms and making phone calls to pre-certify medications that are not automatically covered. There are a plethora of forms for patient's employers or for disability.

As far as I know, there is no rule requiring us to provide any of these services. WE DO 100% OF THIS ACTIVITY FOR FREE! (So much for the doctor always thinking about money when they do an activity or provide a service.) In the past, when a patient had a test done, they followed up with the physician for a billable visit to get the results. That would be an extra co-pay for the patient and payment from the insurance company. We handle this over the phone or by Email, for free. We could ask patients to come in for a visit in order to get all medication refills, which would be a billable service. We could charge people to fill out forms, or make calls to their insurance companies. We could let them handle the fight to get medications covered. There is no law requiring us to provide this service. A physician takes calls at night and over weekends, 24 hours a day, 7 days a week, 365 days a year, including holidays. There is also no law that says a doctor has to take patient's calls at night. We provide that service for free. All of these items probably take up 40% of an offices activity.

Do you still think all doctors are making business decisions when they provide services to patients? Microsoft would go bankrupt if they provided 40% of their activity for free. There is a reason why doctors are notorious for being bad businessmen. A good business person would never provide this amount of care for free. The lawyers certainly don't do it. Every time we call our lawyers for a simple question, it is considered a billable hour. As they are largely lawyers, maybe Congress thinks we bill for these services.

Concerns for the future: If the evaluation of patients is delayed, if the tests are delayed, death and disability are inevitable outcomes. The concerns for the future are too numerous to count in this situation. Medicine has become so complex that it is not possible for the smartest primary care physician or nurse practitioner to be expected to handle or understand all illnesses. With a push away from specialists, will anyone really know enough about complex diseases, which are plentiful? In a government system, the primary care physician may not be able to refer quickly to a specialist. The delay will lead to death in some and unnecessary disability in others.

Those of you who are proponents of socialized medicine may feel this loss is acceptable, and you have a right to your opinion. You can't, however, say that socialized medicine is extending care to more people, as it is not. It is simply shifting the loss of care from one group to another. Anyone a proponent of socialized medicine must also be a great proponent of malpractice reform (not mentioned by the Reformers). You can't expect primary care physicians to make all these complex decisions correctly while limiting their ability to use specialists and tests. Their malpractice costs will skyrocket!

Who is going to provide all of these services your physician now provides for free in the future? When a Government employee works at night, after their usual working day, they get paid overtime. Will I be getting overtime for my hours of call? If not, don't you think physicians will form a union far larger than the United Auto Workers Union demanding better working hours and environments? As revenue to my office is reduced, I will have to let employees go. There will be a huge collateral loss of employees and the ones that provide these non reimbursed activities will have to be the first to go. Patients will get no help with the services that used to be free. This will take huge hours away from their own personal work and productivity. Test delays will lead to delays in diagnosis, further days sick, and an increase in sick leave. This will impact every employer in the United States.

I do not think the Healthcare Reformers understand how offices practice and how health care is really delivered. I certainly know that they have not taken all of the free services into account. The system will cost them far more than they bargained for and rationing will ensue.

Do Specialists Cost More?

I believe this is one of the greatest misperceptions perpetrated by the Healthcare Reformers. They state that specialists order too many tests and do too many procedures and this is driving up health care costs. For instance, they look at neurologists, like myself, and say that we cost too much because we order too many MRI's. The suppositions is that by limiting referrals to neurologists, less MRI's of the brain will get done and we will save money. That supposition is false, and I will explain why.

Why did specialties evolve? Actually, we should add subspecialties to that question as most specialties are so complex, we now have subspecialties. Even at an institution like Harvard Medical School, the Division of Neurology has world renowned experts in many subspecialties that are far from experts in the other subspecialties. You wouldn't want the epilepsy doctor taking care of your multiple sclerosis patients, for example. Diseases became more complex as our knowledge expanded. The more we know about medical science and disease, the more detailed it becomes. The more we know, the longer a physician has to study and train to master the skills necessary to take care of particular patients. If there was no need to train further, i.e. every doctor already knew all there was to know about a specific field, then there would be no need for specialists and sub-specialists. This is not easy, as I have said. Diseases and patients are so varied and complex that it takes years of exposure to recognize and treat certain illnesses.

No matter where you sit on the "reform fence," I think we all can understand why specialties developed over the years. I think we can all agree that Cardiology did not develop to make more money for cardiologists. I think we all can agree that the brain surgeon came about as there was a specific need for surgeons with extra training in this field. Cutting on a brain is different than a heart or blood vessel. It just is and this is not disputable.

In the end, I do not believe these specialized doctors cost more. Let's first look at MRI's of the brain as an example. Why does one need an MRI of the brain? What information does it provide? An MRI of the brain will show us if a patient has a brain tumor. It will show us if there is narrowing of a blood vessel to the brain that could cause a stroke. It shows if there are collections of blood vessels or malformations and aneurysms that are at risk for rupture and could cause severe disability or death. The brain MRI shows us if a person is having strokes. All MRI's show us tissues in the body in great detail. A CT scan is better for bone and is far less detailed with tissues.

To understand why the Healthcare Reformers are wrong, we need to start off with one simple idea. There are a certain number of individuals in the world that truly have these problems, i.e. tumors, malformations, etc... There are a finite extra number of people in the world who have symptoms suggestive of these problems, but will be shown not to have these problems by the MRI. No one will argue that this is a fixed number of people, and therefore, MRI's need to be done on that fixed number. Who orders the test is irrelevant, but they are blaming specialists as we are the ones who order these tests now.

Currently, most primary care physicians and nurse practitioners who have access to specialists will refer people with certain symptoms to the specialist. The specialist then orders the test in the appropriate number of people. When the Healthcare Reformers look at MRI data, for instance, they will see that the specialist orders far more MRI's than the primary care physician. The MRI cost goes under the "cost center" of the specialist and they conclude that limiting referrals to specialists will decrease the number, and therefore, cost of doing MRI's. The truth is that most of the MRI's are actually done for a good reason and needed to be done no matter what. Most of the time this is true and limiting the referral to a specialist will not limit the number of MRI's, it will just increase the number of MRI's done by primary care physicians. Remember, there are a certain fixed number of people that need the test. If "We the People" want to pay to appropriately treat these people and limit their risk of death and disability, we need to make sure these tests get done, no matter who orders them.

There are several other truths not being pointed out by the Reformers. As we have discussed, a specialist understands the worrisome signs and symptoms of the diseases they treat far better than the primary care physician or specialists in other areas. If you do not allow the primary care physician to refer to a specialist, you may actually **increase** the number of unnecessary tests. It only makes sense that a less experienced physician, not knowing the true signs that indicate when an MRI is needed, will order the test for patients with lesser symptoms. It is only natural. A primary care physician may have done 4 weeks of neurology in total and may have seen only a few patients with true neurological conditions. A numb or weak arm can be completely benign, or may be a sign of pending death or disability. The neurologist can have a tough time on occasion differentiating between the two. Just think how tough it will be for a less experienced physician. The knee jerk reaction will be to order a test, like and MRI, just to be sure and to cover the primary care physicians from malpractice suits.

You hear insurance companies and Healthcare Reformers stating that "unnecessary medical testing" is driving up the costs of health care. They define "unnecessary" as any test that comes back negative. Well, the truth is that many tests are necessary but come back negative. If a patient presents with a certain sign or symptom, has the appropriate risk factors, certain tests are indicated. In fact, many of the tests are needed and it would be "true Malpractice" not to perform them. For instance, if a 65 year old male presents with chest pain, he has a family history of early heart disease, he is a smoker and has high cholesterol and hypertension, it would be 100% indicated to do testing to exclude coronary artery disease. This patient, with those risk factors, probably ends up getting a cardiac catheterization as that is the best test for the problem and his life depends on the doctor getting his diagnosis correct quickly. If his catheterization turns up negative, the Healthcare Reformers and insurance industry record this as an "unnecessary test." Any well trained, ethical, physician will order that test 100% of the time. It is necessary, appropriate and the decision has nothing to do with money!

Now, let's reiterate the malpractice issue. If the primary care physician has less experience, sees a mild neurological sign that they are less trained to diagnose, and cannot refer to a specialist to help, what do you think they are going to do under the current medical malpractice environment in America? They are going to order tests that are not necessary in order to "cover their butts." Heck, I do it all the time unless I am 100% sure it's not necessary. In medicine, even for a specialist, it's hard to be 100% sure of anything as people present so differently. So, my rule of thumb is that if there is even a "small chance" of death or disability if I forgo the test and miss something, I do the test. Since I have vast experience in neurology, my definition of "small chance" will be much more restricted than a primary care physician with less neurology experience.

Concerns for the future: The Healthcare Reformers have set out to limit specialists. Although, I will again admit that there are a small number of doctors abusing the system by ordering too many tests, we all have to agree that a fixed number of people need those tests. The tests will get ordered by primary care physicians and they will probably order more than are necessary as they are not as well trained to know when the test is truly needed. Once the Government is in charge, they will need to limit the tests altogether in order to bring down costs. Once they learn that the primary care physician orders as many or more tests than the specialists, they will need to prevent the tests from being ordered at all in order to bring down costs. Many of these tests find treatable diseases that, when delayed lead to death and disability.

The Truth About Medical Costs and Hospitals

Let us again look at medical testing. The supposition by the President's statement on July 22, 2009 was that doctors order tests in order to make more money. The largest proportion of the health care dollar is spent in the hospital. No one disputes this fact. There is, however, a fact left out. Most of the tests ordered by physicians in the hospital provide no revenue for the physician who orders the test. We order blood tests and tests in radiology departments primarily. Some of us order tests in the cardiology department. 100% of those testing dollars goes to the specific department and the hospital. I order an MRI, the hospital charges $2,500 and I get nothing.

In the hospital, most private practice physicians are paid simply to take care of the patient. If they are an employee of the hospital or an academic physician, they are paid a fixed salary. In private practice, we are paid the most in the first 24 hours. Let's use $250 for example as the reimbursement in the first 24 hours. For subsequent days, we make anywhere from $20-40 per day on average. So, the greedy doctor would do best never to have a patient in the hospital more than 24 hours, right? The doctor could then move on to new admissions (to get as many $250 patients as possible) or move on to see more of his office patients. What do you think ordering tests does to the length of the hospital stay? Obviously, the more tests we order, the longer the patient stays and the more money the doctor loses as he or she is handling the lower revenue generating patient. After day 1, ironically, we are incentivized largely not to order tests. Why do we order them, Mr. President? Because it's the right thing to do for our patient's life and wellness and money rarely comes into the decision process. By the way, for the same type of patient seen in the hospital for $250 for 24 hours, we would get paid about $350 in the office. The office visit takes about 30 minutes. Doesn't sound like a good businesswoman should spend much time with hospital patients, does it?

Some of the medical tests done in the hospital cost more than others. Take, for example, the work up of a chest pain. If you have a patient that needs work up of a heart attack, you could wait 24 hours doing cardiac blood enzymes, do a stress test in the next 24 hours, and then finish with a cardiac catheterization on day 3. The catheterization, of course, costs the most. If the Government System required that the enzymes and stress test to be done first, it may actually cost more. Why? Well, the hospital stay gets extended. Instead of a catheterization, treatment and discharge home in 24-48 hours, the patient is in the hospital an extra 2 days and many will get the catheterization in the end. The hospital stay, each day, is the highest expense on a bill. So, for each day wasted, the costs go up. Instead of trusting a cardiologist to use her years of training to recognize when a catheterization is needed, we may force her to follow protocols. As I stated, this could actually increase the cost of care. It could also lead to death due to delay in diagnosis and treatment.

Concern for the future: So, the accusation by the President when it comes to medical care is largely false when it comes to physicians practicing in the hospital. Physicians in the hospital get paid to take care of a patient. Most do not get paid to order more tests. How can the government then limit hospital costs? You guessed it! Less hospital admissions or delay in time to admission to the hospital. That's how it works in Great Britain and Canada. If you make it too hard to get admitted or get the appropriate surgery, many people will end up not needing them because they will die while waiting. Some will get disabled while waiting. Many will be out of work and lose their jobs while waiting for the life preserving surgery.

Physician versus Hospital Reimbursement

Physicians are reimbursed far less than the hospital for the same procedure and for the same treatments. I have given a few examples, but I want to give a few more to drive home a point about costs and how they go up. Remember, the hospitals have GREAT lobbyists in Washington, D.C. Physicians have little to no lobbying effort. When a physician lobbies, it is called "conflict of interest because we have a financial stake in the healthcare system." So, am I to understand that when a hospital lobbies, there is no financial stake in the system?

Many oncology centers developed to treat cancer patients in the oncologist's office. The overhead costs were the space and the staff. Those were added expenses and the treatments that occurred there had to at least equal the added costs. That's simple economics. Most patients enjoyed treatment in the oncologist's office over infusion centers at hospitals. Who wouldn't? These are the people that you and your family have trusted to save your life. They tended to be very comfortable places, not stale like many large hospital cancer infusion centers. Eventually the majority of oncologists had to stop treatments in their offices. While the hospital was reimbursed $1000 for a drug, the doctor was reimbursed $800. These prices were set up by Medicare and were largely influenced by lobbyists. When the price of the drugs went up, costing for this example $900, the oncologist could no longer afford to provide the service. So, if we went from a 50/50 split before the price change, the average cost of the treatment was $900. (Half of the patients were charged $800 at the oncologist's office and half of the patients were charged $1000 at the hospital, for an average price of $900.) After the oncologists shut down their treatment centers, the average price of the treatment went up to $1000, or an average of $100.

I can give countless other examples, but it would take another whole book to list them all. An MRI at an orthopedic surgeon's office costs $500-800, where at the hospital it costs $2500. A spinal tap done at my office costs about $40 after costs are accounted for, while at the hospital it costs over $500. The list goes on and on. If we only do tests and treatments at hospitals, which is the idea of the Healthcare Reformers, the cost of care will go up. Do you think maybe the hospital lobby has been talking to the Reformers? I wonder how much money is being donated to Congressmen and Congresswoman's campaigns by the Hospital Lobby?

Concerns for the future: There is no doctor lobby essentially in this health care reform debate. There are huge hospital lobbies. I suspect that services will be further shifted to the hospital. The cost, therefore, will go up. The whole idea of reform is to bring costs down, right? This shift to the hospital makes the cost of each procedure and treatment go up. When that happens in the future, there is only 1 way to bring costs down. You guessed it, ration and reduce care or usage. People who we could have helped, will go without services. Now we are back to square one. Some get treatment and some don't. The difference is now the Government is "judge and jury" as to where the healthcare dollars are spent.

Paperwork

I commend the President on his promise to decrease paperwork in medicine. It is very true that a huge portion of my day is spent on paperwork. I could be spending this time taking care of patients instead.

Where I disagree with the President is on how the paperwork will change in the future. While it's a good political promise, the idea that the Government will help reduce paperwork is simply untrue, or at least unheard of. In fact, the concept is comical. The truth be told, the Government is largely responsible for the paperwork. Have any of you heard of HIPPA? We commonly call HIPPA, HIPPO, because it feels like the Government induced HIPPA is like adding paperwork the size of a HIPPO on our backs. HIPPA is a monstrosity of regulations and forms added by the Government to make sure your records are private, and yours. Well, at least that's what it started out to be. Before HIPPA, guess what? Your records were yours and yours only. No one had access to them except you and those you authorized. After billions of dollars were spent to set up this program (and continue to be spent on the program) you are no better off than you were before.

There are currently 2-3 other programs being set up to "protect patient information" that will also add to the paperwork burden. Guess what, these programs are not coming from Blue Cross Blue Shield or Kaiser. They are coming from the Government. So, unless you can give me a single example of how the Government has ever stepped in to "reduce paperwork," I will remain skeptical. It only makes sense. The Government is run by laws and lawyers. When a lawyer gets involved, paperwork skyrockets. Have you ever tried to do something as simple as rent a bicycle at the beach? You have to sign a 2 page document.

Remember, it is the Government and Medicare that set up the rules for doctor's notes. They decided the completeness of a note should dictate payment scales, not the degree of time or complexities of a patient. Any rational person would come to the conclusion that the harder the task in medicine, the more the potential complications, the higher the payment should be. That's just common sense. But no! The Government said that's not enough. You need to actually have the exact documentation to go along or you are committing a crime. Yes, a crime they call "fraud" that is punishable by large fines. Remember, if the cardiologist rushes you to the catheterization lab, saves your life, but forgets to write that she asked you how your sleep pattern has been, the cardiologist can't bill for the highest service no matter how hard your case or the procedure that saved your life.

My favorite paperwork story involves one of my group's contract experiences. When the most recent Stark Laws came out, we had to make sure were in compliance. I read the new Stark Law. I downloaded it off the Federal Government web site. It took 80 sheets of paper, it covered both sides of the paper, and each side of the page had 3 columns of small printed writing. We hired a lawyer specializing in Stark Law and the institution did the same. 2 lawyers and $40,000 later, we had a new contract to keep each entity in compliance with the Stark Law. Both sets of lawyers, however, did admit that the Law was so vague and difficult to interpret, it was hard to know exactly what "compliance" meant.

Just say that over a few times out loud and think about it. "The Government is going to DECREASE PAPERWORK." Now think about your tax bills, the tax codes, the forms for your car from the Department of Motor Vehicles. Try not to laugh as you then say again, "The Government is going to DECREASE PAPERWORK." I bet you can't say it with a straight face!

Generic Medications and Your Pharmacy

All doctors agree that if 2 drugs are equivalent, the cheaper should be prescribed. The generic drugs are usually cheaper and no physician has a problem with a generic prescription if they are equivalent. Many new drugs are improvements on older or generic drugs. If they are better, if they will have a better impact on a patient's outcome, we want the newer drug to be used. If they are better just based on side effects (for instance, less nausea) then most of us have no problem with the generic being tried first. If the side effects are overwhelming and the patient has given the drug a valid effort, then the newer drug with less side effects should be given. That is generally how physicians approach medications in 2009. The physician makes no money based on the medications they prescribe, neither generic nor name brand.

Those of you with insurance with pharmacy benefits have heard of a Formulary. The Formulary usually has 3 tiers. You get tier 1 medications for the lowest price, tier 2 for a higher price and tier 3 at the highest. Then, of course, there are drugs that are not on the Formulary which are not covered at all. Naturally, you would assume that the Formulary takes the cheapest, equally effective medications, and puts them on tier 1. The next cheapest goes to tier 2, and so on. You would naturally assume that if there are 10 generics for the same problem (like hypertension) they would all be covered and on tier 1. Well, this is not necessarily the case. Most insurance companies contract with a drug supplier, not directly with the manufacturer of the medications. The drug supplier gives a deal on a whole group of drugs for every medical condition. Therefore, if you have seizures, your tier 1 seizure medicine was bought because it came with the package of all the other drugs, like hypertensive medications. Maybe your seizure medicine is actually the most expensive seizure medicine available, but was bought with a cheaper group of hypertensive medications, or vice versa.

What happens when your doctor has had you on an inexpensive seizure medicine (based on true manufacturer cost) which has helped your seizures for years, but the Formulary actually places that medicine on tier 3? Well, you could switch to the tier 1 medicine, right? Your doctor has correctly informed you that any time you miss or switch your seizure medication, you are at a higher risk of having seizures. You know that having a seizure will preclude you from driving for 3-12 months. You know at worst that a seizure may lead to your own death or death of others (for instance, if you are driving while you have a seizure). Quite a dilemma, right? You are at the whim of the insurance companies' contract with the drug supplier, even though your seizure drug would be the cheapest if bought directly from the pharmaceutical manufacturer. Wouldn't it be nice if drugs were directly purchased from the manufacturer and not through a "middle man?" Maybe even the patient could call the manufacturer directly because the drug is actually cheaper than the tier 1 drug on the formulary.

Generic medications are legally allowed to differ from the name brand by 15%. So, if you are switched to a new generic blood pressure medicine, you simply monitor your blood pressure for a week or so to see if it works as well. If the pressure goes up, it likely won't go so high that it causes a stroke or heart attack. If it goes too low, you could pass out, but that's not likely. If your seizure generic medicine is higher than the prior name brand, you might get lethargic and fall asleep while driving, but it's not likely. If your new generic is too weak, you might have a seizure. Big Whoop! You've had seizures before, what's one more going to hurt? If you are driving when this happens and run through a school yard with kindergartners playing, oh well. If the generic saves money, for society, it's a price we must be willing to pay, right?

Maybe, just maybe, knowing more about the patient and the condition the doctor is treating would be helpful when mandates are made about the medications patients are allowed to take. Would it make a difference to know that the seizure patient had many seizures on many different medications, but the one they are currently on has kept them seizure free for 5 years? Would it make a difference to know before changing the hypertension medication that the patient had very difficult to control blood pressure and has had hypertensive strokes before? Would it make a difference to know that the patient on an anti-depressant tried to commit suicide many times before their current medication was prescribed? Every patient's history and set of risk factors are so very different. Doctors make medication decisions for many reasons. I have no doubt that it's more cost effective to just give the cheapest drug available. But, there are many characteristics, specific to each patient, that come into play when medication decisions are made.

Side effects are a real issue. If the side effects are not tolerable, it does not matter how effective the drug is on controlling a disease. I am 100% sure that we can all agree on the following statement:

a drug works only when it actually gets into the body! Many new medications have far fewer side effects. If a patient fails a generic due to side effects, they should be allowed to try the newer medication. Also, a medication that has a generic formulation, can actually have 10 or 20 different manufacturers. These different generics can, therefore, differ from each other by 15% and still meet FDA regulations. However, each time the pharmacy or insurance company changes the generic to a new manufacturer, the patient is at increased risk of side effects and lack or effectiveness.

All physicians have a problem with a pharmacy, with a pharmacist, making changes from a name brand to a generic without the authorization from a physician. Because, as stated above, generics can differ from one another, we have a problem with one generic being switched to another without our permission. In the end, if the side effects come back or the effectiveness wears off as a patient goes on a new generic, the physician is responsible for the new problem. Are you aware that pharmacists and pharmacies are often rewarded financially when they change your medication to a generic or from one generic to another? A name brand medication can cost them, for instance, $50 to purchase and the insurance company reimburses them $60. They make $10 in that transaction. If they sell the generic form, or switch to another generic form, it may cost them $10 and the insurance company reimburses $40. They make $30 in that transaction instead of $10. The pharmacist may actually have a mandate or may get a bonus from corporate headquarters based on how many times he or she makes a change like this. They are directly rewarded financially for the change to a new form of a generic or to a generic from a name brand. The generic can change month to month based on the deal the pharmacy chain makes with a drug supplier.

Talk about conflict of interest. This is done only for financial reasons for the pharmacy, with little to no knowledge about the specifics of why the patient is on the drug to begin with or what other complicating factors exist in the patient's history. If the patient has a seizure that leads to death or disability, if the patient has increased depression and commits suicide, who do you think is liable in a lawsuit? The Pharmacy? No, the physician. Even if the physician warned the patient that a change in medications could lead to such a bad outcome, the patient can sue the doctor. I tell 100% of my seizure patients that this can occur, yet I am still liable if the pharmacist makes a switch without my approval. Do you think the pharmacies have a better lobby in Congress than physicians?

CHAPTER 10

Real Patients, Real Decisions 2009

Ted Kennedy- Brain Tumors

I did not take care of Ted Kennedy, nor did I speak to anyone about his case. What I know is from the news. My understanding is that Ted Kennedy had an incurable brain tumor called a glioblastoma. The life expectancy for someone with this type of tumor is 12-18 months with aggressive surgery, radiation therapy and chemotherapy. My experience with similar patients is that they are not normal for 18 months, then suddenly die. Their memory, personality, and ability to function deteriorates steadily. In the last 3-6 months, many of these patients are non-verbal and are completely disabled. Mr. Kennedy had the best doctors in the World taking care of him at Mass General, the NIH, and Duke University. An enormous sum of money was spent on his care, despite the fact that his fate was certain the day the diagnosis was made.

Why do I bring up Ted? Well, he made a statement, when his mind was still sound, that was very misleading. He said that he was getting the best of care for his disease and he wanted to make sure the same treatment would be available to everyone. Well, there are 2 realities hidden in that misleading comment.

First of all, the members of the Federal Government, like Senators and the President, have a separate health care system. The current health care proposals exclude their health plan from the new system. That means, their health plan will not change with the new health care system. What's good for the US people apparently is not good enough for the politicians in Washington, D.C. I suspect that other groups will also get excluded based on their donations and lobbying efforts, like the United Auto Workers Union.

Secondly, with the proposed health care reform measure, we clearly will have to ration care. Someone with a glioblastoma will NEVER get care the likes of Ted Kennedy. This is an incurable disease. The only care these people will get is through NIH funded research trials or morphine to keep them comfortable. There is no way the new plan allows hundreds of thousands of dollars to be spent on the last year of a life with a 100% mortality rate. For the second lie, many proponents of socialized medicine may agree. Why spend that kind of money on an incurable illness? That's a fine position to take, but understand that the statement by our Healthcare Reformer, Ted Kennedy, was in fact misleading and non-factual.

Concerns for the Future: Certain populations of people will get better health care based on political affiliations. This is kind of like Communist Russia. You will need to align yourself with a Federal Government job or a powerful union in order to get care like we provide in the 2009. This opens up a whole political "can of worms" and forces more dependence on the Government. Unfortunately, most of the US population won't have this affiliation and will get sub-optimal care as financial resources diminish for the health care system.

A lot of the American people I talk to just feel that it will be no big deal. You will be covered more cheaply by the Government. If you need a test, a better drug, or a procedure that is not covered, you will gladly go pay for it yourself. Well, this happens in some countries, but not many. In fact, it may actually be illegal to get care not specified under the Government or individual plan. In countries where this occurs, there is care done "under the table." There might not be a monetary exchange, but gifts and services can be provided instead. Let's face it, if the CEO of Coke wanted to get seen by me and the waiting list was 8 months, I am sure he or she would somehow get to my office in a quick fashion. So, that's great if you are a CEO, a politician, or you are "well connected," but that isn't the case for the majority of the US population. Will the NFL player with a torn ACL get put on a 3 month waiting list to see the orthopedic surgeon? I doubt it. I suspect the NFL Players Union will be exempted from the new healthcare system and will have its own system like the politicians.

Now remember, the Government will be controlling supply and demand. Let's again use the MRI for example. Let's look at Ted's hypothetical non-political friend who needs an MRI (supposing he had one or two non-political friends). If he is wealthy, but the MRI waiting list is 3 months, what is he going to do? Well, he's glad to pay whatever it costs to get one sooner. If he's a billionaire, he'd pay anything. If he's a working class person, he might pay $1000. Right now, MRI's cost about $500 in a private facility and $2000-5000 in a hospital. When they change the health care rules, they will outlaw MRI's in all doctor's offices and eventually in private facilities in order to appease the hospitals and their lobby. Well, although the demand for MRI's will be forced down (the Government will not allow many), the supply will go down even further. Therefore, the costs of the MRI will go up. So, Teddy's friend may be alright with the new costs of MRI's, $10,000, but most US Citizens will not. If, on the other hand, MRI's were on every street corner, the cost would plummet to a few hundred dollars and everyone could afford them.

Unfortunately for most US Citizens, many countries with government involvement in health care, make it illegal to obtain medical services above or beyond what is covered. That's why many Europeans with money travel to Dubai to obtain life saving procedures. Where are we going to go? Not Canada. Maybe the Castro's will get smart and set up some cash paying clinics in Cuba. Just think about it; a 100% cash business. We can put a medical facility in a resort in Cuba. The family can drink tequila and enjoy the beach while the patient recovers from bypass surgery. In places like Dubai, this whole package can be given for about $10,000. That includes the surgery from world class surgeons, airfare and hotel. (Ok, they don't have water sports included in Dubai, but Americans will want their water sports, so Cuba will add this to the package.)

Seizures

I received a call from one of my colleagues in internal medicine. Dr Z. is one of the smartest internal medicine doctors I talk to and he only calls me with true perplexing neurological cases. He was taking care of a 50 year old professional with lapses in his concentration. People at work were limiting his activity as they were concerned about him making mistakes. Dr Z., again being very smart and given the patient's very atypical behavior, ordered an MRI of the brain. He was concerned about the patient having had a stroke or a brain tumor.

When he told me the story, it sounded like the patient was having seizures. I had heard this story many times and had seen many patients with the exact same symptoms. When I asked Dr. Z. specific questions about duration of these events and what the patient's colleagues witnessed, it was quite clear that these were seizures.

I asked Dr. Z. what the MRI showed. He stated it was "non-specific" but there was something noted in the left side of the brain (more specifically, the temporal lobe). Now, Dr. Z. is extremely smart, but he is not trained to read an MRI and did not look at it himself as he wouldn't have known what to look for. He was dependent on the report which essentially gave a list of possibilities of what this brain finding may represent.

Due to modern technology, as I was talking to Dr. Z., I was able to pull up the MRI on a computer link to a hospital radiology department and look at it directly. This abnormality on the MRI was clearly a small blood vessel malformation and was in an area of the brain that often caused these types of seizures. I told him to start the patient on a seizure medicine that day and refer him over for me for evaluation, which occurred within 24 hours. He was informed that he could not drive for 6 months, per Georgia State Law.

So, in a matter of a few days, a very educated internal medicine doctor saw a patient and ordered an appropriate test. He was able to call a specialist and have the correct diagnosis made immediately with a specialist physically looking at the MRI and listening to the history.

Let's look further into why the tests and interaction were necessary. This patient needed an MRI in a quick fashion. He could have had a treatable tumor, stroke, or brain infection. His symptoms were recent, so the work up was urgent. Without the tests and diagnosis, this patient could have had a seizure while driving and injured himself and others (possibly killing others). Seizures can themselves lead to death. The medications have significant side effects, which also can be life threatening, so management by a specialist is appropriate.

Concerns for the Future: This is a case where clearly testing and referral to a specialist is indicated. The potential threat of missing this diagnosis and treatment, the threat of inappropriate management, is life threatening to the patient and others around him or her. What happens if the MRI is delayed? What happens if the internal medicine doctor does not have a specialist he can call to review the MRI and history right away? What happens when this patient can't follow-up with the specialist, stops taking the medicine because of side effects, and has a seizure while driving during rush hour?

How long will it take for an internal medicine doctor to order an MRI or refer to a specialist? How might this impact patients and society? Right now, I am happy to "work in" a patient when a physician calls if it is important and life threatening. Will I be allowed to do so in the future?

Complex Patients

Mrs. T, a 36 year old mother of 3, was admitted to a small hospital in Georgia. She had been diagnosed with multiple sclerosis a few months prior and started on one of the conventional multiple sclerosis medications. Multiple sclerosis is a disease in which a person's own immune system attacks the brain and spinal cord. In essence, it causes inflammation and wages a series of sequential attacks. These attacks are usually spaced over time and every person has a different frequency and severity of attacks. The prognosis is therefore variable, but about 50% of patients will become disabled, or have difficulty walking within 20 years. Multiple Sclerosis is one of my group's areas of expertise, or a subspecialty. We, therefore, see the hardest to treat patients. We see the ones with which even the specialists are not comfortable.

Mrs. T had an aggressive form. Very few doctors in the country know how to treat multiple sclerosis and an even fewer number treat aggressive forms of the disease. Mrs. T was one of the unfortunate people who had such a severe case where the attacks were almost constant and ran rapidly through her brain and spine. With continued conventional therapy, Mrs. T would have been permanently disabled and likely would have died of pneumonia or blood clots within a year.

We accepted her on transfer to our hospital where Mrs. T was started on high doses of chemotherapy and immune suppression. Remember, MS is a disease where one's immune system is ramped up to attack oneself and does so by inflammatory attacks. So, in aggressive patients like Mrs. T, immunosuppressive drugs (like cancer drugs) are used to shut down the immune system. High doses of steroids are also used to attack the inflammation as steroids are a potent ant-inflammatory drug. This can be a risky process.

It is well established and accepted by the FDA, that patients with MS should be provided typical MS drugs. As stated, these work in about 50% of patients. MS is a rare disease. There are no studies that are FDA approved that look at patients like Mrs. T. There are none now, and there never will be. The population is small and there will never be funding for such a large study required by the FDA for approval in a drug package labeling. Many MS Centers around the world have done small studies but none with the typical placebo-controlled model or size to satisfy the FDA regulations. The treatment received by Mrs. T is well accepted however in the MS community, although various protocols have been used.

Mrs. T came over to us on a ventilator, she could not mover her arms or legs, and she had a feeding tube in her nose. Her brain MRI showed massive amounts of inflammation and there was involvement in her spinal cord as well. With conventional therapy, she would have soon died. Well, we still see Mrs. T in our clinic now 8 years later. She is a happy mother with some mild weakness and some memory dysfunction. She is still married and is active in her children's lives.

We have many similar stories as we have used this protocol on many patients. The hospital stays are about 3 weeks and then, due to the severity of disease, a 4-6 week stay in a rehabilitation center usually follows. This treatment is not always successful, but very often stops the aggressive attacks enough that restarting conventional therapy is all the patient needs thereafter.

My other favorite story was about a younger woman. She had gone from talking to being dependent on a ventilator within a few weeks. After her treatment, her parents took her for rehabilitation in a nursing home, in her home state. She was still on the ventilator and had a feeding tube placed in her stomach. She was hardly able to move her face, eyes, or arms and legs.

After about 6 months, we started to get pictures from her. First they were pictures of her friends visiting her at home, with her sitting in a chair. The pictures then became much more joyous. They were pictures of her out, at restaurants and clubs, socializing like a normal 20 year old. About a year and a half later, she was back in our town, working full time and living independently.

Concerns for the future: Well there are several problems with such patients in the future. There are many common diseases where people progress in a more rapid fashion or things happen differently than the norm. Remember that no two patients are exactly the same. Physicians will always have to deviate from standard therapy for these patients or they will die or become disabled. No formal studies will ever be done on a large enough scale to give FDA or Government approved statistics. As it stands now, small studies are done, patient series are developed and the physician often needs to talk to the insurance company in order to explain a deviation or more aggressive treatment. The insurance companies almost never say no. We can get through to their medical director the same day. With socialized medicine, there is no easy to reach government official to contact. If there is an avenue to alter therapy from the government protocol, the process is slow and results are worse as the therapy is too late. Instead of reaching a medical director at an insurance company, there are medical review boards set up by the governments. You cannot reach these Boards easily, and certainly not in a day.

We also hear a lot about decreased referrals to specialists. Well, I am one of about 6 neurologists in the entire State of Georgia that feels comfortable with this type of aggressive multiple sclerosis. I am an adult neurologist, but I will even treat children with this aggressive disease because even the pediatric neurologists have too little experience in these cases. My hospital is allowed to take these kids or adults on transfer for me to treat. Will that be allowed under the new system? Can we really expect them to allow transfers to a sub-specialist in a life threatening case when they don't even want specialists around?

The truth of the matter is that it is probably more "cost effective" for the country to let Mrs. T and the 20 year old die. Right now, I look at the individual patient. I decide if the patient warrants this type of treatment; sometimes they do and at other times they don't. In socialized medicine, we look at patient populations and disregard individual cases. When do we decide that the patient is not viable and when we should stop all treatment? Right now, I look at each patient and the facts surrounding their condition. I stop once it is clearly futile. I continue to treat when there is a realistic chance that I can still help someone. For every patient with inflammatory brain disease, to the point that they are on a ventilator and require a feeding tube, only a certain percentage of people will survive the aggressive treatment. Fortunately for Mrs. T and my 20 year old patient, they were ones that survived and went on to live productive lives. The United States we know and love does not disregard individuals and feels compassionate to take care of those in need.

Emergencies and Emergency Rooms

We already discussed how the government may intervene to save money by limiting hospitalizations. People get admitted to hospitals in one of 2 ways. Either they are sent in directly from a physician's office (this may also be a scheduled admission for a test or procedure after seeing the physician) or they come through the emergency room. The emergency rooms and physicians who serve them are already largely overwhelmed. The ER physicians are trained to recognize and treat life threatening emergencies. They are also trained to recognize patients with illnesses that require an admission versus those who could be sent home and treated in the near future by outpatient physicians. This is not an easy job. Much to the contrary to what insurance companies and Reformers will lead you to believe, the ER physician's job is almost impossible. Sure, there are some cases that are "textbook," some are handled emergently with a gut instinct, and some are so minor, they require no thought process or testing.

The great majority of people who come into the ER require a thorough history, evaluation, labs and other testing before the ER physician understands the next step. Many Emergency rooms are overcrowded now with people who use their services as they would a primary care physician. That is, they have no regular doctor, they just go to the ER when they have a minor ailment. I wonder how this will change in the future. The Reformers talk about everyone having a primary care physician to avoid using the ER instead. I certainly see how providing all people with primary care physicians would decrease more expensive ER care in many cases.

In the future, other patients may be shifted to the ER for care. For one example, what will the patient do that needs to see a specialist, has a numb or weak arm, and who is now on a 6 month waiting list to see the specialist? What does the patient do who I tell has a risk of becoming paralyzed, who I tell needs an MRI? What is the patient to do when the waiting list is 6 months and I warn them they need an MRI in 2-3 weeks? I don't know many Americans that will take that risk and wait in line for the specialist or MRI. They will get scared and go to the ER (if I don't just send them there myself to avoid a malpractice situation). I see there being an obvious shift of one type of patient out of the ER and another into the ER. This will negate the benefit of everyone having a primary care physician in order to remove the over-use of the ER.

A few weeks ago, I heard an ER doctor call into a radio program telling of his conversation with a member of the House of Representatives. The ER physician complained that about 75% of all the tests ordered in the ER are unnecessary and are ordered out of fear of malpractice. Essentially, the tests are ordered for what we call defensive medicine or CYA medicine (cover your ass medicine). The Representative told him that he did not believe malpractice was an issue and that ER physicians order such tests to "make more money." Well, let's examine this misconception that we have heard several times from Reformers (including the President). The majority of ER physicians are salaried employees; they, therefore, make no extra money by ordering tests. The hospitals might, but the physicians don't. The ER physicians will be stuck ordering even more tests because they will have the liability if they send the patient home and something bad happens.

Concerns for the future: Let's examine several assumptions. If ER physicians order tests for CYA reasons and they are not reforming malpractice, how are we saving money in the new system? If ER physicians don't really make more money now by ordering tests and they do so largely to CYA, then where is the incentive to limit tests in the future for an ER physician? If I am correct that there will be a shift of the types of "unnecessary" patients overusing the ER, how are we saving money by providing everyone a primary care physician? The ER physicians will now be ordering MRI's and more expensive tests for patients who are too concerned to wait on the longer waiting lists. ER physicians are not specialists or sub-specialists in the hundreds of areas of medicine they see, so they will be afraid of missing illnesses.

I would be happy to examine the proof or a previous example of how this assumption by the Reformers was successful at saving money, without rationing care of course. I don't think I will see one, as it does not exist. I hate to see the Government banking on unproven assumptions gambling with our tax money, our physicians and their choices, and our lives. No matter what they pass, it will be an experiment if they drastically change the way we practice and receive health care. With such risky possible outcomes, it just makes sense to a simple mind like mine, to do things slowly if one really wanted to change healthcare for the better.

Unnecessary Hospital Admissions

Label me "guilty as charged." Let's examine why a physician would admit someone to the hospital that they knew didn't have a reason to be there. I probably do it 20 times a year. I probably consult on another 100 patients a year that are admitted unnecessarily by another physician. That's just one physician in one hospital. I already explained how I lose money in the hospital and how I would make more money seeing the patient in the office. So, why do I do it?

I can give you a story that I have heard and a patient type I have seen a hundred times. The Emergency Room calls me to see a young person, age 20-40, who presents to the ER complaining of a sudden onset weakness. My hospitals have acute stroke protocols that quickly gets such patients triaged and fully evaluated in case we can provide a life altering medicine or procedure. Such a patient could have a stroke, a brain tumor, or a vascular malformation. They could also have a psychogenic process where there is absolutely nothing physically wrong. It is very common for stress and other psychiatric illnesses to present in the form of a stroke. A heart attack is another common presentation and the story is the same.

Over the phone, I can't tell if it's physical or mental, so I go quickly to the ER. Very often, I can tell right away that there is nothing physically wrong. Because I have seen thousands of people who truly have strokes or brain tumors, because I have done thousands of exams on patients with these real physical abnormalities, I can often tell just by talking to the patient if it is psychological. I have been practicing for 9 years, after training. I have seen thousands of patients in each of those years. To date, I have been wrong twice when I thought the patient had nothing wrong or was "faking." That's 2 out of thousands.

What do I do when someone presents with what I believe is a psychiatric process or is "faking it?" Most of the time, I admit them for the stroke work up at the tune of about $10,000. Is this cost effective? No. Do I want to admit them? No way! I know that in all likelihood, the patient could be sent home and followed up as an outpatient and the system could be saved thousands of dollars. So, why don't I send them home? Well, I have a whole lot to lose personally if I send them home and nothing to lose if I admit them to the hospital. I do not pay for their health insurance that will pay the hospital. I do, however, pay for my malpractice insurance. I also will pay dearly in time away from the office and my other patients if I am sued. A law suit leads to countless hours away from patient care. I lose the law suit every time if the patient is the 1 in thousands where I am wrong, even if I my reasoning is sound based on my exam, initial findings, and experience.

Now remember again, oh ye Reformers, that I do not gain financially by admitting this patient to the hospital. I get no money for the hospital stay, the MRI, or the diagnostic tests. The hospital does. I make the most money the first time I see the patient in the ER, about $250. No matter what happens after that initial evaluation, the subsequent days of care pay me about $20-30 for each encounter. Each patient in the hospital on subsequent days takes about 30 minutes of my time. The office patients take about 15 minutes of my time and pay the same amount. You do the math. Each subsequent day I go and see the patient in the hospital, I lose far more revenue than if I was in the office.

Concerns for the future: Well, since there is little to no talk about malpractice reform, I see no reason why I will admit less of these patients to the hospital. Unless I am 100% sure there is nothing wrong and the patient readily admits that there is stress causing the symptoms, I will continue to be forced to admit the patient because I can't afford to get sued.

Where is the incentive for me to trust my judgment and take on a risk by sending them home? Until society allows physicians to be wrong without getting sued, why should I risk sending the 1 in 10,000 home without a work-up? I document everything I do and everything I am thinking when I see a patient in the ER. If my reasoning is sound and if the majority of reasonable doctors would have come to the same conclusion, will it ever be permissible in the US to be wrong? I don't see it in the near future.

So, if the Reformers are banking on changing my behavior in the ER as part of their "healthcare savings," they again are in for a rude awakening. The costs will be much higher than they are projecting and they will have to ration care.

Stroke

About a third of what a neurologist sees in the hospital are patients being evaluated for a stroke or TIA. A stroke occurs when the blood supply in a part of the brain is shut off and part of the brain dies. A TIA is a "transient ischemic attack," which means the patient had a stroke and the symptoms quickly resolved (either the blood supply was restored or the damage was so minor, the patient's symptoms went away). Both stroke and TIA patients need the same work-up and have the same risk of a recurrent event in the first 30 days.

The work-up involves an emergent CT scan of the brain. This enables us to tell if the patient has had a bleeding stroke, which has a higher mortality risk and may require emergent intervention. The patient then gets an MRI looking at the brain and the blood vessels that supply the brain. This shows the stroke or tells if there is any damage. This tells us if there are blood vessels that are threatening to close off or require intervention. The CT scan does not show us much except for bleeding or very large stroke. The CT scan costs a few hundred dollars, the MRI costs a few thousand.

Most patients require an echocardiogram (or ultrasound of the heart) in order to see if the blood supply was cut off by a clot that came from the heart. The patients are admitted to the hospital, usually for 1-3 days, during which time the heart rhythm is monitored continuously. The heart can be going in and out of a rhythm that causes clots to go back to the brain or cause another stroke. Each hospital day costs $1500-2000. The echocardiogram costs a few thousand also. In some patients with particular presentations, we also do blood testing to see if they have genetic predispositions to stroke or if they have another medical illness that caused the stroke.

Why do we do these tests? Well, it's not for a physician's financial well being. The tests help us determine how to help the patient recover from the current stroke and how to prevent any in the future. Once someone has had a heart attack or stroke (both vascular events), they are far more likely than the general population to have another. The tests help us determine if the patient will do better with some surgical procedures (like a new heart valve) and they tell us which medication is best. Not all the medications for stroke are equal or indicated for everyone and they all have risks. We don't want to place every stroke patient on Coumadin, for example. Coumadin has been shown superior to aspirin like compounds in a few causes of stroke only. It also adds risk of bleeding (possibly bleeding to death) and interacts with many foods and other drugs.

I do not know how to put a number of the cost-effectiveness of these procedures. I can tell you from experience, that less than 20% of the tests give me information that changes the way I treat the patient in the end. In essence, many of the tests are negative, a small stroke is seen, and I would have guessed correctly the first time I saw the patient. The tests, more often than not, do not alter the way I treat the patient. However, for the other 20%, the tests really, really matter. Is this cost effective? Do I spend way too much money affecting the lives of a few? It depends on whether you are asking one of the 20% or a politician.

The cost effectiveness of the stroke work-up really is a personal question. It is very personal for those whose lives I have saved and extended, especially the 20 year olds. One of my first patients whose life was forever altered by a stroke was a 20 year old female. She was talking a little funny one morning, but otherwise looked normal. Her boyfriend thought she was just joking around and let it go on for a few hours. The young woman then called her mother who became alarmed right away and brought her to the hospital. The CT scan looked fine. The MRI of the blood vessels looked fine. The MRI of the brain showed 2-3 strokes. None of the blood testing or heart monitoring was abnormal. However, her echocardiogram showed a clot sitting on one of her heart valves. Her condition was called marantic endocarditis and needed to be treated with surgery on her heart valve. Without the surgery, the strokes would have continued, disabled her and eventually killed her. The tests, therefore, saved her life. She had a 2 year old girl at home at the time of the stroke. She went on to have a functional life and kept working and taking care of her daughter. (I don't know what happened to the boyfriend.)

So, for my 20 year old patient, I know how important she feels it is to keep doing all these tests, even though most of them will be negative. Is it more cost effective to let a small percentage of people die and become disabled to save money? I don't know if it's cost effective, but I do know that it's un-American and unethical in my opinion.

Now my 20 year old story was a little too easy. Let's make this a little more difficult for the Healthcare Reformers. Right now, I pretty much do the same work-up for a suspected TIA or stroke no matter what. The blood tests may be different based on other medical conditions or age. (The inherited traits, for example, present under the age of 50, so they are not necessary in a 70 year old.) The treatments may differ as well. For example, a patient who had a previous life threatening bleeding condition from coumadin does not get this drug as an option. Many of these patients have a stroke and their symptoms are gone or extremely mild by the time I see them in the emergency room. To the world, they look good enough to go home and get the work-up as an outpatient. This would save thousands of dollars. I keep them in the hospital because I am armed with a well known statistic. Of those patients who go on to have a second stroke or progressively get worse, they are going to do so in the first 48-72 hours. Very often, a patient will get worse, have a second event, or have a complication within the first 12 hours of their hospitalization. I often can have a major impact on their outcome because they are in the hospital and not at home. If I was doing this "for the money," I would advocate sending all these people home. The ER or primary care physician could just send the patient home and they could follow-up with me in the office. I could bill for an initial visit and not have to bother going over to the hospital to round for 2-3 days.

Why does this example give Healthcare Reformers difficulty? Many countries with socialized medicine will not admit these patients at all; some will not admit these patients if they are over a certain age. This, to them, is more cost effective. I can see their point. If no one over the age of 65 is allowed repair of their cardiac valve, why keep them in the hospital to look for the problem? The same can be said for the genetic blood tests in young patients who have strokes. I take care of about 10 patients that had positive tests. They are on lifelong coumadin. Coumadin, again, is not entirely safe, but they are far more likely to die without it. I have seen hundreds of patients under the age or 50 who I have ordered the blood tests on and they came back negative. It was only helpful in those 10, so I doubt the tests are "cost effective?"

Sometimes after watching a patient in the hospital for a day or 2, I feel comfortable completing a patient's work-up as an outpatient. If my stroke patient is stable, there MRI does not look worrisome and their heart has looked stable, sometimes I feel comfortable sending the patient home and getting the neck ultrasound or echocardiogram as an outpatient. Let's say, for example, the patient comes in on Thursday night and the echocardiogram won't be done until Monday. If they are stable enough and the conditions are right, I will order the tests and get them done Monday or Tuesday as an outpatient. The savings are about $1,500 per day just for the hospital stay on Saturday and Sunday.

Right now I have no problem doing this because I CAN get the test done in a few days. I make one phone call and my office sets up the test. They may need to call around to a few facilities to get the test done quickly, but it gets done. What happens in the future when outpatient tests take too long to get done? What happens when the outpatient routine waiting list is months long? I need these tests done in days, not weeks or months. I will be forced to keep these patients in the hospital longer and this will cost more money. When the system loses its efficiency, it will cost much more.

Concern for the future: I can give countless other stories of patients whose lives were saved because we aggressively worked up strokes. Not all of them are young. In fact, most of them are older than 65, a common age for treatment cut-off in socialized medicine. I have taken care of countless patients who have had surgery on their hearts and blood vessels to the brain over the age of 65, 75, and even 85. To date, the oldest was a gentleman who had surgery on his neck blood vessel at age 95. He had 3 consecutive strokes over a month before the surgery, despite maximum medical care. He had a plaque (or clot) in the blood vessel and he would have clearly died soon without the surgery. He recovered and survived another 5 years. Was that cost effective? The family and I were allowed to decide what was best for him, not based on a government making decisions about a population or a budget. There is not a single insurance company that practices in the United States that would have stood in the way of that surgery. A US Government run system will most definitely stand in the way, maybe not in the beginning, but certainly within a few years.

I Treat Everyone the Same

I have not once ever looked at a patient's insurance or asked their financial status before I came up with a treatment plan. Sure, when someone calls my front desk for an appointment, they review the insurance information and tell them if the visit will be covered. If they have no insurance, we let them know what the costs will be and discounts that we are legally allowed to offer. If I walk into an examination room in the office and the patient has no insurance, I am unaware of that fact unless they bring it up. Certainly when I come up with a treatment plan, if they have no insurance, we discuss how I am going to accomplish the patient's needs and fulfill the necessary goals. We discuss payment plans, we set them up with social workers, we look for free resources to get the patient medications they need.

When I am in the emergency room, or get a consult in the hospital, I never look to see if the patient has insurance. I proceed with the testing and treatment, use my education and experience, and proceed with an appropriate plan of care for that individual. I also don't evaluate the patient's ability to "contribute to society" or if the patient inflicted the illness on themselves. I take care of many patients in our hospitals who have caused their own illnesses. For instance, my patients with cocaine induced stroke, kidney failure and heart disease get the same treatment as any other patient.

Concerns for the future: I tell you this not so much because I think that will change, but to show you our mindset (again, the purpose of this book). It may be true in the future that I will be forced to treat people differently based on a scale of "worthiness to society." I may not be able to do testing on the patient at age 70, who has never smoked or drank, and takes care of herself with regular diet and exercise, simply because of her age. I may be able to do all the tests I deem necessary on the 30 year old with a cocaine history, who has developed self inflicted kidney disease and cardiac disease, leading to her stroke. I think this is the more likely scenario. Remember, socialized medicine is all about populations. Statistically speaking, a 30 year old will produce more for society than a 70 year old. When you have to spread a limited resource (medical care), you have to set arbitrary parameters. When you take out the individual's needs and characteristics, you focus on the population as a whole. We may not go "socialized," but when the government sets up a "Board" to decide how health care is given, populations and statistics will be used to distribute care. The money for such a Board already came in the first Stimulus Package by the President and the Board is part of the legislation being drafted now, at least in the House of Representatives. I don't know how the health care bill will eventually look, but I do know that this Board is coming (and here to stay).

Spinal Stenosis, Walking and Age

I had been following a very pleasant 77 year old female for about a year with a complaint of dizziness. She was otherwise very healthy.

She presented one Monday with leg weakness, clearly an unrelated condition. Her friend, a physician, recommended she call me after she mentioned her symptoms the day before. She called Monday morning, explained the symptoms to my front desk, and was booked onto my full schedule the same day without any problems. Since her symptoms were new and concerning, my staff understood that she needed to be seen quickly. She explained that over the prior 2 weeks, it had become increasingly difficult for her to walk. She was using a cane now and was having trouble getting around and taking care of herself. When I questioned her further, it became apparent that she had intermittent left leg numbness for about 6 months and chronic, manageable low back pain.

For her dizziness, I had sent her to a balance and physical therapist. They had worked on her walking. It is not unusual for a 77 year old to have difficulty walking for a variety of reasons, so naturally the therapist gave her exercises to maintain her leg strength, which she performed religiously.

Her leg weakness and numbness would increase with the distance she would walk, was worse going upstairs, and she noticed numbness when she would sit for a long period of time. This was an easy diagnosis for me and took very little thought. I knew right away what was going on, what needed to be done, and how quickly it all needed to happen. She had lumbar spinal stenosis, or narrowing in the lower spine, likely due to degenerative disc disease. The appropriate initial management for this was physical therapy (which she already had). For patients displaying progressive weakness like her, surgery is indicated. She needed an MRI of her lower spine and a referral to a spine surgeon.

Despite her age, this woman needed surgery. The MRI could be done in a few days to a week, unless she continued to get progressively worse, so she didn't need to go to the hospital. I arranged an MRI in less than a week and she had a surgical appointment the same day. This took 2 phone calls to an MRI Center and a surgeon. The surgeon knew me well and understood it was urgent whenever I called. My secretary made these 2 calls and I had to make one more call myself. Her insurance company wanted to get more details as to why this was urgently needed. The medical director agreed with me in a discussion taking less than 30 seconds.

By the way, this 77 year old female still worked full time for a local bank. She was retired from a major corporation, where she served as an executive, lived alone, and enjoyed staying active at work and in the community. Without surgery over a 2-4 week period, she ran the risk of getting progressively weak, not being able to live independently, and becoming dependent on others (both physically and financially). She was able to get seen immediately, with one phone call, to her specialist. She was able to get the appropriate test and surgical evaluation within a week. She was able to remain fully employed, fully active in the community, and to live independently.

I would estimate that 50% of my patients with suspected low back or neck narrowing never get an MRI. Of the 50% that get an MRI, usually because of concerning weakness, only about 10-20% ever go on to get surgery. Most of the patients are treated with physical therapy, medications, massage or chiropractic therapy, or treatment by a pain specialist. Every patient I encounter is told that if I feel they need surgery, all conservative measures will have failed first. They understand that when I recommend surgery, they have a concerning symptom or exam finding that pushes me to that recommendation. My income never plays a role in the consideration. The most appropriate, least invasive, and most convenient treatments are all that enter into the decision process.

Concerns for the future: I suspect that rationing of healthcare will limit or eliminate the ability to do MRI's in such cases based on age, regardless of the patient's independence and function. If the system comes close to Great Britain, the waiting list for an MRI, even if I can get one on a 77 year old female, will be months out. This patient would have become permanently disabled prior to the MRI being performed in that case. The MRI may show a surgical process, but it may take too long to get her in to see a surgeon or the surgery will not be available due to her age. Finally, if I feel this is urgent, I am concerned that I won't be able to talk to a Government sponsored medical director to get the procedure and surgery approved quickly.

Those Darned Expensive Tests

I saw a 40 year old gentleman who had recently suffered from a stroke. In one arterial territory on the left side of his brain, he had a moderate stroke. When I saw him, a few months after the stroke, he had an almost normal exam. His right sided weakness was gone and his language deficit was gone as far as anyone on the street would be able to tell.

He was sent to me by his local neurologist for a second opinion about further treatment. His echocardiogram revealed a small hole in the heart between the left and right atrial chambers. 15% of the population has these small holes, essentially remnants of the heart when we are all developing as a fetus in our mother's belly. On rare occasions, they are the causes of strokes. I was able to look at his MRI of the brain and blood vessels. Interestingly, he had a narrowed blood vessel to the left side of his brain. A week before his stroke, he was chopping wood. Actions like this can cause a tear in the arteries in the neck which can lead to stroke. We treat them with coumadin for 3-6 months and then switch to aspirin like compounds once they are healed. This patient was on coumadin out of concern that the stroke came from the hole in the heart. There is debate, but lifelong use of coumadin is considered a treatment option for patients suspected of having strokes coming from this hole in the heart.

The decision process got a little more difficult. The MRI does not conclusively tell you if the artery has a tear. This patient had a history of radiation therapy 10 years prior on his neck for a tumor, from which he recovered. Well, radiation can also cause a narrowing in the neck arteries to the brain and they can look indistinguishable from a tear on MRI. A tear requires coumadin (which again has major risks) while radiation induced narrowing simply requires aspirin. Now remember, he also has a whole in his heart that can be normal or can cause strokes in rare cases. This often requires lifelong coumadin or a cardiac procedure to close the hole. We had to take all of this in consideration deciding how long to keep him on coumadin with all of its dangers.

Now, let's get back to testing and money. I ordered a type of CT scan of his left vessel (called a CT-Angiogram). This is non-invasive and is very sensitive at picking up narrowing versus tears in the arteries. Oh, by the way, it is also done in the hospital and I receive no compensation for the test. I could have simply seen him for one visit, taken my payment, and moved on to the next higher paying new patient. I could have told him to go back to his neurologist after 6 months of coumadin, by which time the vessel should be healed if it was a tear. Done and simple, right?

Well, what if he bled to death over those 5 months on coumadin? Would it still have been alright to take that approach? That approach never entered my mind because the patient's best interest was the only thing on my mind. Since I, as almost all physicians, think only for the benefit of the patient, the whole idea that revenue is a factor is insulting.

It turned out it was a tear. It was caused by the chopping of wood and the risky coumadin was indicated for 3-6 months. It was in his best interest to stay on coumadin for 3-6 months, not just switch to aspirin, despite the risks coumadin posed. This helped us forget about the hole in his heart. A surgery on that hole was not indicated and we could relax about it being anything more than a normal anomaly seen in 15% of the population. (By the way, his cardiologist from the hospital also told him not to worry about the hole. The cardiologists group does, in fact, close these holes at a hefty price. The cardiologist, like me, never thought of money when he treated this patient.)

Concerns for the future: There are many concerns here. Second opinions by specialists are almost non-existent in countries with socialized medicine. The Healthcare Reformers have made it clear that they want to limit referrals even once to specialists and reward primary care physicians for treating as much as they can alone. Therefore, first opinions will become limited. In this case, a specialist required another specialist's opinion since he had more experience. How can a primary care physician be expected to keep up with the ever growing medical knowledge and take care some of the difficult cases? Well, they can't.

What happens in the future if this patient is not allowed to be referred to the specialist, or sub-specialist? What happens in this country when this patient has a complication of therapy when there are other tests that would have pointed treatment in the other direction? Once the complication occurs, more tests, or a post mortem exam, may show that there may have been an error or the treatment was not necessary. Even thought the primary care physician may have followed protocol set forth by the Government in a patient's care, our medico-legal system will leave that doctor as a "sitting duck" with no chance to legally defend themselves.

It is clear that some States are far superior to others in malpractice reform. Heck, in some States there is no malpractice reform. Many of these States are also, coincidentally, the most expensive in which to live. What do you think is going to happen to doctors in these States under the health care reform proposed? Well, let's see. My cost of doing business is going up. My reimbursement is the same or going down.

I am limited in how I treat patients, but am liable for their lives and outcomes anyway. The cost of living in my State is going up. THEY WILL BE UNABLE TO PRACTICE IN THE STATE AND WILL BE FORCED TO LEAVE. I predict some States will have doctors who are only employed by hospitals, none in private practice. As they struggle to get quality physicians, the quality will go down. Good luck New York. Good luck Washington, DC. (Oh well, at least the politicians will have good doctors as they will be exempted from the healthcare system they create.)

Migraine Headaches

As a neurologist, I take care of a large number of patients with migraine headaches. Actually, I initially went into neurology because I had really disabling migraine headaches as a child. I became more interested in helping patients with brain and spine abnormalities restore normal function, so I decided not to specialize only in headaches. Over 50% of the population has had at least one headache that would be considered a "migraine headache." These are not mild, by definition. They are moderate to severe in nature and involve disabling pounding pain with nausea and sensitivity to lights and sounds. In a proportion of people, these happen frequently. Unfortunately, they can completely disable a person temporarily while they have headaches. In a small proportion of people, they are so frequent and so severe, that they interfere with any daily function **all the time.** These people can't work, can't participate in family activities or activities with their friends, and they become functionally disabled.

I am a specialist. I obviously don't have people come to see me with mild headaches. My patients have severe headaches and they have already had a disruption in their lives. They usually have already been tried on over the counter medications as well as several common prescription medications for migraine headaches. Patients do not come see a headache specialist for fun. They come for help because the headaches are severely interfering with their lives.

When someone comes to see me, we review their types of headaches, what might be the triggers, and what medications have been used already. We do a thorough evaluation of how they took the medications. Many people don't take them correctly or do not give the medication enough time to help. Treatment for migraine headache includes avoidance of triggers, over the counter medications and supplements, and then prescription medications. When the prescription medications fail, there are intravenous therapies and injections.

We may hear the politicians say that the "headache centers" cost more than the general internal medicine doctor because the "headache centers" use the expensive intravenous and injectable medications. In fact, the President's statement in his July 22nd speech would lead you to believe that the doctor at one of these centers would base his treatment decision solely on the revenue he or she would generate from the procedure. He did not just imply it, he made the direct statement.

This simply is not true for many reasons. I can promise you, as a physician who deals with migraine headache sufferers and uses all forms of treatments available, we have only 1 agenda when we see the migraine sufferer. We want to know how we can treat this person the simplest and never have to see them again because they have been cured. Most of the time, we understand that we will have to see them more regularly than "never again," and we want them on a simple regimen to function with little to no pain. The revenue of our treatment regimen NEVER comes to our mind. We use the more invasive interventions not to make more money, but because the other treatments have already failed.

Let's remember how a patient gets to a headache specialist. Most patients don't want to go to a headache doctor's office just for fun. They go out of necessity. They first have headaches that are disabling. Many are having problems missing work or daily activities with their family and friends. They have been to a primary care physician who has tried many regimens. Still their headaches stop them from working and having fun. Some may be having problems in their personal relationships as their partner can't really sympathize with them. I mean come on, how bad could a "headache" really be, right?

Concerns for the future: It is obvious that the patients that go to a "headache center" are the worst of the worst. These people don't respond like most people. They need the more aggressive therapy. When the Healthcare Reformers look at the costs attributed to the center, it looks high. They will look at the cost, not care about outcomes, how much better the patient does, nor how the return to normal function leads to increased productivity in society. They won't look and calculate how many of these patients failed other routes, many lifestyle changes and many medications.

What will happen when the patients can't see a headache specialist? What will happen when they can't even see a neurologist with extra experience with migraine headaches? How many people will lose their jobs, lose their spouses, and lose vital experiences with their children because the extra treatments that could cure them are just not available? Healthcare reform will alter the supply of these treatments. I can promise you, the patient demand will not change. A physician once said to me, "the hardest neurological disease to treat is migraine headaches." I didn't know what he meant at the time, but I understand now. I know exactly what to do for a patient with a stroke, a brain tumor, of even a progressive incurable disease like Lou Gehrig's disease. These diseases plateau or end. Migraine sufferers are all different and they have an incurable disease that lasts a lifetime. We have numerous options and each patient responds differently. Once we get rid of their headaches with one regimen, the same headaches can come back later becoming refractory to the successful treatment.

Fortunately for me, my migraine headaches went away. I have had 2 in the last 20 years. I have patients who get 20 per month or even have them daily. Without specialists and procedures to treat them, will we just let them become dysfunctional? I suppose that's cost effective. Let's just hope that you, your loved one, your friend or your co-worker aren't one of those intractable migraine sufferers.

Pain Centers and Procedures

Pain Management has become a whole separate field of medicine. It follows the same story as the migraine headache centers mentioned above. This subspecialty developed not because some doctors realized they could perform procedures on people and they would make more money. The truth is that the specialty of pain management exists because there are a large portion of patients that are in need of advanced pain techniques and medications. The medications available have increased. The risks of these medications have increased and should, therefore, be used only in specialist's hands. These medications are extremely addicting and can ruin a person's life if used improperly.

The procedures to cure or limit pain have greatly increased as well and, again, require extra training.

At pain centers, 100% of the patients are referred in from an outside doctor. The pain specialists do not go looking for patients in need. These patients have all failed routine treatments. The pain physician does a full evaluation and offers up suggestions to get rid of the pain. Often this requires interventions that cost more money than simply adding a medication. The procedures can be one time events that can cure the patient's problems. Medications are more "lifelong" and are more risky with more long term side effects.

It is my understanding that the Government, especially Medicare, is looking closely at ways to limit pain centers because they are "expensive." Let's remember that there are a certain number of people in the world that need these procedures or medications to function. Getting rid of the "pain center" does not limit the number of people who need the center, just the availability of the center to those in need. It limits the number of people who will get proper treatment "in order to save money." No internal medicine physician will ever be able to do these procedures, so people will suffer.

Now, let's remember that the people who need a pain center are not "bad people." These are not drug seeking people for the most part. They are people, like you and me, that have injured their spine, joints, or bones often in a car accident or fall that wasn't their fault. Medicare is interested in getting rid of the centers to save money. The elderly, whose only evil was to get old and develop low back pain, will not have access to this care. They will be left disabled as they cannot see a specialist that could cure their pain. They will be left in wheelchairs or, even worse, their beds.

Let me tell you about a friend of mine who is not elderly. He is in his 40's, has a regular job, and is a very productive person in society. He rarely gets sick. However, for unknown reasons, every once in a while he will "throw out his back." He will be laid up in bed, unable to work or function. This can last up to 6 weeks, taking high doses of ibuprofen and oral steroids which are medications that increase the risk of perforating his stomach and bleeding. He has had this happen 2-3 times and it always follows that course. Fortunately for him, he was once referred to a pain specialist for this problem. With a single steroid injection in his low back, he is back to work the next day. Now, I guarantee the bill for the injection is much higher than generic ibuprofen and steroids, but I also guarantee it costs society a lot less keeping him at work and functioning. I also guarantee that anyone in his shoes would be glad such procedures exist. I am sure his company is happy he's not out on short term disability for 6 weeks every year or two.

Concerns for the future: My concerns have already been stated. If we look only at the costs of pain specialists, we are missing the big picture. The need for such specialists exist, i.e. there will always be a certain percentage of people with these types of pain that can be cured or improved by these specialists. The Healthcare Reformers are only looking at the cost and not the benefit. People like my friend and many of my patients will be left to suffer. Many will become truly disabled and even more will become functionally disabled as they are dependent on narcotic medications.

Let's again just reiterate how crazy it is to demonize the pain centers. That's what you will hear when they take them away. People need a service in order to live a normal life or stay at work. We have the ability to help these people in a specialized medical center or with a specialist. We will say that these centers are too expensive and require these people to be treated by untrained physicians. A large proportion of these people are the elderly. They will be left to wheelchairs and beds, requiring someone else to take care of them. Is there a price to pay for these centers? Yes. Is it worth the price? Again, it depends on who you ask. I am sure if the Chief of Staff at the White House develops back pain, 1 day off from work instead of 6 weeks off makes a big difference and is worth the money.

Reversing Dementia

All readers know that when a person has Alzheimer's Dementia, there are no cures. Doctors can only slow down the process. Dementia is a very costly disease, both financially and mentally. The financial costs of taking care of a loved with dementia can be staggering as they require supervision 24 hours a day. The emotional toll and disruption of a families' life is not measurable.

When a patient comes to see a doctor for memory loss, all doctors will look for symptoms or a history that point to one of the few reversible causes of dementia. One of these is neurosyphilis (or tertiary syphilis). When someone is exposed to syphilis, through unprotected sex, they can contract the syphilis spirochete (an organism like a bacteria or virus). This spirochete can live in the body hidden for years. When it comes out later in life, it can have profound effects on the brain and spine. It can be tricky to diagnose. Some patients present like they have an acute meningitis (or brain infection). Some can present with atypical stroke patterns or patterns of spinal cord compression making it difficult to walk.

One of the presentations that is more commonly seen is a form of dementia. These patients tend to have a problem with memory that progresses slower than a stroke, but faster than an Alzheimer's patient. When any person presents with this pattern of memory loss over the age of 30 or 40, with a past history of unprotected intercourse (even once), neurosyphilis is considered as a potential cause. Fortunately, if it is detected it can be treated and cured, unlike Alzheimer's Disease. As a rule of thumb, the earlier it is detected and treated, the better the recovery or cure.

The diagnosis of neurosyphilis as a cause of memory loss is made eventually with a spinal tap. Before a spinal tap is considered, one does a blood test to detect prior exposure to syphilis. Spinal taps are uncomfortable and rarely can be dangerous. They should not be done on everyone with memory loss as there is risk and neurosyphilis is a rare disease. There is one blood test called an RPR. This is cheap and done by most labs. However, it is normal in over 50% of patients with neurosyphilis. There is another blood test called the FTA. This test takes longer, is often sent out to a special lab, and is more expensive.

When I was in training, I became an expert in neurosyphilis after an experience with a great person/patient. While in the neurology clinic, I saw a man with a chief complaint of memory loss. He had served his country for 30 years. He had a photographic memory and had learned 3 languages while serving in other countries. He was an avid reader and never forgot anything he read. He was married and still working at age 60 when he started to lose his memory. He had unprotected sex before marriage. His memory had been declining for about 8 months and he was no longer able to work. I looked at his records in the VA computer system. He had a normal head CT scan and all his labs were normal, including an RPR. I did not see that an FTA was sent.

His primary care physician was one of the smartest doctors I had ever worked with before. After the CT scan, labs and RPR were negative, the patient continued to decline, prompting the referral to the specialty clinic. I asked the physician why he had not sent the FTA, only the RPR. It turned out an FTA was ordered but, since the test was more expensive, they would only send the RPR. The VA required a referral to the neurology clinic before they would allow the FTA. So, the physician ordered the referral. 4 months later, he showed up on my door at the neurology clinic. The patient had gotten much worse. He could no longer read and make any sense of what he read. He was only able to speak English. The FTA was sent, was positive, and he then had a positive spinal tap.

He did get the proper treatment, 5-6 months late. He did respond to the antibiotics, improved, but the delay cost him memory that he would never get back. He lost memory and abilities that could have been prevented with the correct blood test being sent right away. He never returned to work.

Concerns for the future: This example gives several concerns for the future. The VA functions much like socialized medicine. They look at a fixed amount of money and decide where it should go. They are not thinking of my patient whose memory and life could have been spared. They look at the global population they are treating and decide which diseases and tests they feel are needed. In my practice, I am able to think just about the individual and treat accordingly. That's why my patients come to see me.

The other concern is in specialty care. In my current practice, we do not like to have patients wait more than 3 weeks to come see us for a new appointment. I will always work late to see someone sooner if it is specifically requested by a physician. It took 4 months for this gentleman to get from his primary care doctor to a specialist. The delay cost him some of his brain function. It is well documented that in countries like Great Britain, it can take 6 months or more to see a specialist.

There is no doubt that in the future, US health care could be run exactly like the VA. Tests that could be done to save lives or cure illnesses will be refused "for the greater good." Specialists that could figure things out right away will be difficult to see. I have said this before, I am not trying to change your opinion about how health care should be delivered. This is America and you have the right to your own opinion. Just accept the fact that socialized medicine shifts treatment from one place to another at the wishes of a governing board. People will still go without care, without proper care, and will still die and become disabled from illnesses that medicine and doctors could have prevented or remedied.

Right and Left Hand Numbness

A 30 year old single mother of 3 was referred in for consultation by her primary care physician. She complained of numbness in both hands. (I did not go out looking for her. I did not advertise looking for anyone with hand numbness so I could make money.) She first noticed this problem during pregnancy about a year prior. It would only occur once in a while and did not bother her at all.

That part of the story was not unusual, as women who are pregnant often get carpal tunnel syndrome. If that was the end of her story, she would have required no further testing. We could have given her wrist splints to wear at bedtime if the symptoms returned. There would be no need to order nerve tests. In a case like this, testing could give me an answer as to what was going on, but would not alter my plan.

Well, her story turned out not to be this simple. For the prior 3 months, she was not really able to sleep. When she would lie down, both arms would ache. The symptoms involved all 5 fingers on both hands and both arms up to the neck. If she sat up, the pain would go away immediately. She started to feel that her arms were weak. Her exam, however, was completely normal.

Fortunately, her primary care physician recognized that her story was a little different. Fortunately, the physician was able to refer her to a specialist and get her seen quickly (in less than 2 weeks). Statistically, a person with a story of numbness in both hands has carpal tunnel syndrome, which is not emergent. However, this complaint can also be a sign of pending disability if not diagnosed and treated immediately.

Her symptoms, above the hands and the positional nature responding immediately to sitting up, are much more likely to indicate problem with the spinal cord. There can be a compression from a herniated disc or a mass in the neck region. Rarely this can represent a cancer near or in the spinal cord. Multiple sclerosis or fluid in the spinal cord are also possible. These are conditions that must be diagnosed and treated promptly or disability is a real possibility. A compression on the spinal cord is the most urgent. As a rule of thumb, when a person has surgery to relieve the pressure on the spinal cord, whatever their exam looks like at the time of surgery is what it will look like permanently. Some people improve, but the promise to them is that they won't get worse. So, the longer it takes to make the diagnosis and treat with surgery, the more function the patient loses that they may never get back. Someone with paralysis from a cervical spine compression has about a 10-15 year life expectancy depending on how high up and how severe the weakness, therefore, we try always to prevent paralysis.

I was able to order an MRI of the cervical spine (neck). The test was done within a few days. It took NO phone calls to the insurance company. They saw the diagnosis request of "cord compression" and didn't question my judgment or diagnosis. She did have a herniated disc (likely from a car accident when she was a teenager). She underwent surgery a week later and has no weakness or numbness. Her surgery was performed by a neurosurgeon. I received no money for the referral or surgery. Her MRI was done at an independent facility, so I received no money for the MRI. My objective was to get her MRI as soon as possible, at the facility with the shortest waiting list, so I could take care of her as quickly as possible.

She still has a normal exam, feels normal, and has a normal life expectancy. She is able to continue working full time, taking care of her 3 children as a single mother.

Concerns for the future: The Healthcare Reformers are talking about specialists and tests like they are evil. I am not sure if this type of person will get to me in time to prevent disability in the future. She likely would have worsened over a few months (if not weeks). Once the compression reaches a critical level, the damage would have been irreparable. In the future, even if I see some of these patients on time, will I be able to get the MRI quick enough to make a difference? If the MRI is done on time, will the back log for surgery be so long, that some of these patients will become disabled while waiting for surgery?

There are problems in healthcare in this country, but no one can argue that the efficiency and speed of the system is second to none and saves lives. We take for granted how quickly the system works. When the Government gets involved, like in the VA system, things will move much slower. No one can argue that point as ALL GOVERNMENT RUN SYSTEMS ARE SLOWER. Slowing things down, decreasing the number of tests done, will decrease the number of people treated. Even if the primary care physician, the neurologist, or the surgeon recognize the problem on time, if the delay set up by the Government leads to disability, who is liable for the lawsuit? You don't think the extended family of the single mother of 3 won't advise her to sue someone when she is disabled, do you? How is she going to take care of the 3 kids? Even if the patient understands that the doctors did nothing wrong, a lawsuit will still occur. You can't sue the system or the Government, so you sue the doctor.

I have some facts that you should put in the "it's crazy but it's true" category. I am not making this up. This is directly from MAG Mutual, the insurance company that caries most of the liability insurance for physicians in Georgia. As soon as the patient or the primary care physician sets up an appointment at the specialist's office, the specialist is liable for that patient. Let's say my mother of 3 gets a referral, calls my office, and sets up an appointment for 3 weeks later. All my office knows about her is that she called with symptoms of hand numbness. We call her 2 days before to confirm her appointment, and she says she'll make it. She decides the day of the visit that she's too busy to come. If she goes on to become disabled, the specialist is liable and can be sued. According to MAG Mutual, we had established a relationship with that patient when we scheduled her appointment and it is our responsibility to make sure the correct services are provided. Even if she comes and we tell her she needs an MRI, we scare the life out of her as to what the implications are for cord compression, if she decides not to get the MRI we are liable if she gets disabled. Now, we are not expected to follow patients to appointments. However, we are responsible to "make every effort and document those efforts" to make sure the patient comes to the office for her visit and follows through with any tests of treatments we recommend.

We are about to enter an era, possibly, where the reimbursements to physicians are going to go way down. There is no mention of malpractice reform, so our liability won't change. Our chances for malpractice will skyrocket as they will limit our ability to do tests or refer to specialists. If we are also responsible for tracking our patients, there tests, and their compliance with our recommendations, the system will cease to function. We have 10 physician equivalents in our offices. We all see an average of 20 patients a day (on slow days). That's 200 patient encounters a day. How many extra employees do you think it would take to track the appointments with us, the tests we order, whether or not the tests are done, and whether or not the patients followed up with the treatments or referrals outside our offices? Remember, these employees don't work for free. They have salaries and benefits. Even today, this is a strain with the current revenue to our practice. We essentially told MAG Mutual, "thanks, but you might as well ask us to cure every form of cancer, today!"

Again, for those interested in socialized medicine, I just want you to understand what you are asking for. I also want you to understand that the current Healthcare Reform debate can't possibly be just about fixing the system to provide care to the uninsured. If it was, malpractice reform would have to be a large portion and it is not being mentioned, AT ALL! You can't have a true health care reform debate without talking about malpractice reform.

Left Hand Pinky Weakness

Most of us could probably get by with a little weakness in our left pinky. Now don't get me wrong, I like the pinky and I understand it's needs and uses. However, if I had a choice of one finger to preserve, it would be the thumb and not the pinky. Now, if my job required the use of the pinky as equally as the other fingers, I might have a different opinion. Let's say, for instance, if I worked for a symphony orchestra playing a wind instrument, I might have a different opinion. If my income came entirely from playing music and teaching others how to play instruments, I could see how the loss of the pinky might be problematic in many ways. That would be very true if I spent years of training to get to the highest level of playing (the symphony orchestra) and really had no other skills to make a living.

Musicians can develop problems with their nerves. I see patients who develop a "musician's dystonia." These dystonias are actually a problem derived in the brain. A more well known form of this is "writer's cramp." People with these dystonias have the inability to control their hand as they take on a contortion or spasm every time they try to write or play an instrument. Obviously, for someone who plays at the level of the symphony orchestra, this leads to a complete disability as missing a note really matters. Just think how Tiger Woods would play if every time he gripped a club his left hand and wrist cramped and contorted. While it might not affect my golf game, it certainly would for a professional like Tiger.

Often these dystonias can look a lot like something else by history and exam. One particular patient I saw had difficulty moving his left pinky when he tried to play an instrument. This was getting progressively worse and would render him disabled very soon. I wasn't sure, based on his exam, if he had a true musician's dystonia or if he had a entrapped nerve across his elbow. I did, however, have a test that could answer the question. Also, the results of the test would drastically change my treatment plan, and his life forever. If it was an entrapped nerve, surgery could potentially cure the problem and relieve the pressure on the nerve. He likely could keep playing and working. If it was a dystonia, there would be little one could do. Rest may help along with some medications, like Botox, but he would definitely be out on disability for at least a year.

The test, called a nerve conduction test, was performed that week. It showed a compressed nerve across his elbow. Because of the implications of him worsening and losing the ability to do what he loved to do, his sole source of income, we referred him to a surgeon. He had an operation within a month of seeing me on consultation. He continues to work as a musician and is not on disability.

Concerns for the future: I was dealing with a patient who needed a test and treatment in order to prevent him from becoming disabled. Just like my spinal cord example, the longer you let a nerve lose function, the less likely you are to see return of function. What would have happened if it took him longer to get the referral to see me, if it took longer to get the nerve test, or if it took longer to get the surgery? What if the referral, test, or surgery are not in the health care plans of the future? Well, these patients will become disabled, 100% of them.

This is an example of a condition that no one, other than a neurologist, can diagnose. If a primary care physician is required to treat this or diagnose it for 6-12 months before they can do a referral, then the diagnosis will be missed 100% of the time. This is not a knock on primary care physicians. They are trained to do things that I can't do. I am able to make certain difficult diagnosis only because I have the extra training and I have seen thousands of patients with nerve entrapments.

I did make more money doing the test. However, I did not order the test to make more money. I did not order an MRI of his elbow even though I would have made more money doing so. An MRI would not have helped with his diagnosis, nor treatment. I ordered the appropriate test because, #1 it was going to tell me something I didn't already know and, #2 it was going to change the way I treated the patient for his benefit. The only financial considerations when dealing with him were the amount of money he would lose if he could no longer work. The entire accusation that money comes into play when I interact with patients is just simply incorrect and insulting.

I have said many times in this book that if the Reformers believe they can save health care dollars by removing physicians financial incentives to do tests, they will find out they are wrong. The only way they will then be able to save money is by limiting the tests. This is rationing for everyone, even for those that could have been saved by tests. If my patient had come to me 6 months later, the costs of our interaction would have been reduced. They would have saved about $3,000 for the test and surgery. The insurance company would have saved money. Why? Because in 6 more months, his muscles from that nerve would have been so diminished (atrophied) that the diagnosis would have been obvious. I would not have needed the test, because his exam would have made the diagnosis easy. The surgery would not have helped at that point either, saving the surgical costs. However, the cost to his disability insurance company would have been overwhelmingly higher. The cost to his life and the cost to the Government would have been much higher because he would have been disabled from his profession and dependent on others.

We need reform that still allows the system to function like it does today. We need to be able to diagnose and treat, where indicated, as quickly as we do now. If the system becomes more like socialized medicine, you must all realize you will pay more and get less efficient care in the end. You don't expect me to know how to run IBM. How can you expect a Congressman or Congresswoman with no experience in patient care to understand how to fix the problems or run a whole new health care system? The savings they are counting on won't exist, the system will cost WAY more than they expected, and rationing will have to occur!

The Mother-In-Law, the Knee, and the Orthopedic Surgeons

My mother-in-law now lives around the corner from me. She moved down here from the Northeast about 3 years ago. She has knee pain on both sides, has very little to no cartilage in her knees, and is functionally limited by knee pain. Stairs are difficult. She goes out about once a day and tries to limit what she does physically because of the knee pain. She does not want surgery, unless it is a last resort. She is a good candidate for knee replacement. She is relatively healthy otherwise and would be a very low surgical risk.

She has been seeing orthopedic surgeons for her knees for about 8 years. 2 surgeons were in New Jersey and 2 are in Georgia. So naturally, when she was referred into see each one, they looked at her knees and thought, "This will be great; just think how much money I can make if I operate on both knees." Did that happen even once? No. But that's what the Reformers want you to believe, right? The surgeons are supposedly looking at my mother-in-law as a fee ticket and will do whatever they can to make the most money.

This did not occur with any of the 4 orthopedic surgeons she saw. Instead, they treated her as they were taught during medical school and residency. They treated her like they treat every one of their patients. They evaluated her as an individual, looked at her individual problem, and gave her options for treatment. They took into account her living situation and her desires. They understood that she was smart enough (as most of our patients are) to understand her choices. My mother-in-law does not want surgery. She has worked with her surgeons to treat the symptoms as conservatively as possible. Not a single one of them tried to push her to surgery. Every one of them agreed, given her desires and situation, that surgery should be a last resort. They educated her on the symptoms that would indicate when surgery was necessary. Absolutely 0% of the orthopedic surgeons she saw made a decision that was financially based. Are there some out there that would have? I suspect so. Are they the majority or a significant proportion? I think not!

Concerns for the future: My mother-in-law has been fortunate enough to avoid surgery. She is now over 70, but was in her early 60's when the symptoms started. In the future, I am concerned that age will be a limiting factor for care (aka. rationing). Maybe, if similar patients do the right thing to avoid surgery in their 60's, they won't be eligible for the surgery in their 70's when they NEED it. Maybe these patients will become home or bed bound. It is my belief that the current Reformers predict just that. The Reformers are discussing provisions of home nursing. Why? Could it be that we are predicting the need for more home nursing? We can't expect families who work full time to stay home and care for every bed bound patient in the future. Are we expecting an increase in the number of home bound patients perhaps?

I hope this does not occur, but I am skeptical. My mother-in-law probably needs surgery in the future. The question is, will it be allowed when she needs it? If it is not covered by the new system, we it be legal for her to pay cash and get her knee replacements that will allow her to continue to function independently?

CHAPTER 11

The Future of Health Care

As I stated in the beginning, there is not a single physician who doesn't believe the system is broken. We all support health care reform. We almost unanimously believe that our current health care is the best in the world. When you take into account what we are able to do, how beneficial the technology has become, and how quickly we are able to diagnose and treat patients, it is second to none.

The purpose of this book was to debunk the myth that physicians, in any significant numbers, do things for personal financial gain and add significantly to the cost of health care increase. If you salary every one of us, it will have little to no impact on the costs of the system. In fact, if you shift all the revenue away from physicians, as detailed above, it will raise costs. Physician reimbursement is dwarfed by reimbursement to institutions, like hospitals, for the same tests and treatments. The overwhelming majority of physicians make recommendations that are specific to the patient's risks and needs. The overwhelming majority adhere to the Oath, "First of all, do no harm." When the President or any of the Reformers state otherwise, I take it as a direct insult and it is personal. After all the years of personal, family, and financial sacrifice to learn how to heal people, I am insulted. After the many hours I give daily to take care of the details that affect my patient's lives, I find those comments a "slap in the face." Unlike a lawyer, I do not bill patients by the hour and do not receive any money for a large portion of the time

I provide for the patient's benefit. I believe an apology is deserved, but I don't expect one.

People fall through the cracks in our system now. People will fall through the cracks later. The rules and regulations in the healthcare industry have removed a free market from the system. The rules have removed simple economic principles called supply and demand. The 2 most important people in the system, the patient and the physician, have been removed from all decisions on how the system functions. We are now in a system where we are uninformed consumers. These rules came from where? You guessed it, the Government. Who influenced their decisions when making the rules? You guessed it; lobbyists from the Hospital Association, the Trial Lawyers Association, the Pharmaceutical Industry, and the Insurance Industry.

It looks to me that the Healthcare Reformers are not trying to simply improve the system. They appear to be trying to recreate the system. It is a gamble, to say the least. It has never worked before, ANYWHERE! They are using numbers and statistics that are in many cases not correct, and they are using numbers that are at best guesses. It is well understood that the Government always underestimates costs and overestimates savings. Why does anyone believe it will be different this one time, when our very lives are at stake.

The Reformers are going to make decisions that will limit care. In the first Stimulus Package under President Obama, they provided money to create a Board that will review health care procedures and delivery to decide what is "proven to be effective." They will provide care only for what's proven effective. Well, "proven" and "effective" are certainly grey areas that can be interpreted differently by different people. So, what happens when the costs are far greater than they predicted? What happens when the saving don't exist or amount to enough? They will have to ration care. People will still fall through the cracks, it's just that the Government will define the cracks.

Don't we already have several models to prove that my concerns are valid? The VA system is bankrupt and extremely inefficient. Medicare is bankrupt. Are we just ignoring what our experience in those systems has taught us? The system can still stay private, stay the best in the world, and be fixed. If we worked to improve what we have, change some regulations and allow the patient to become more active in the process, the system could be saved.

In 5-10 years I plan on writing a similar book, one about the way we practice medicine in 2015 or 2020. My predictions are detailed in this book. We will be able to see if my predictions and my distrust in the Government prove to be correct. We will see what happens to similar patients 10 years from now. I trust my patients and their decisions, not an elected official who knows nothing about the rules and finances of the health care system.

Maybe we will get lucky. Maybe things will change for the better. Unlike a politician, I am always willing to admit when I am wrong. No matter what, physicians will still be acting in the best interest of patients, whether they are handcuffed by regulations or not.

If anyone feels the need to send an apology my way for insulting my career and integrity, please feel free to send a letter to my Atlanta office. I promise to pass it along to my fellow physicians.

References

Herzlinger, Regina; Who Killed Health Care; McGraw-Hill, 2007

Herzlinger, Regina: Market Driven Health Care; Perseus Books, 1997

Waters III, William; 2 Days That Ruined Your Health Care; Logikon Press, 2008

The Physician Perspective; Medical Practice, 2005

American Medical Association, 2001, 2005

The Association of American Medical Colleges, 2008

Krauthamner, Charles; The Washington Post; 8/14/09

Nuwer, M, et. al.; E & M Coding; American Academy of Neurology Annual Meeting, Miami, 2005

Kletke PR, Emmons DE, Gilis KD; The changing proportion of employee physicians: evidence of new trends; AHSR FHSR Annu Meet Abstr Book, 1994; 11: 68-9.

ABOUT THE AUTHOR

Dr. Jeffrey B. English is a graduate of Boston College and Dartmouth Medical School. He practices in Atlanta, Georgia where he is in private practice. He also holds a position at a non-profit organization that takes care of patients with multiple sclerosis, The Multiple Sclerosis Center of Atlanta. He is the Director of Clinical Research at the Center. His practice interest focuses on the restoration of function in patients with diseases of or injury to the brain, spinal cord, and neuromuscular system. He has been intimately involved in non-profit care as well as the economics of the health care system. He has given numerous talks nationally on the subject.